Imprint

First Englisch Edition 2024
Copyright © 2024

All rights reserved.

No part of this book may be copied or reproduced. The content is protected by copyright law. You are not allowed to use, share, or translate any part of this book without permission from the publisher and the author.

TABLE OF CONTENTS

Foreword	6
Introduction: The Wheel of Dharma	8
Happiness: The Search for True Contentment	11
The Secret of the Laughing Tiger	12
The Song of the Silent Stream	15
The Dance of the Wind	18
Inner Peace: The Silent Lake Within	21
The Enchanted Temple Ruin	22
The Monkey and the Quiet Lake	25
The White Stone of Peace	28
Self-Acceptance: The First Step to Liberation	31
The Flower Amidst the Stones	32
The Unadorned Mirror	34
The Garden of the Self	36
Compassion (Karuna)	38
The Monk's Song	39
The Elephant's Tears	41
The Petrified Garden	43
Kindness (Metta)	46
The Song of the Forgotten Garden	47
The Animals' Feast in the Valley of Dhara	49
The Singing Bamboo Grove	52
Moralityand Ethics (Sila)	54
The Unseeded Field	55
The Riddle of the Sacred Pond	57
The Song of the Jungle	59

Joy in Others' Well-Being (Mudita)	**61**
The Riddle of the Temple Painting	62
The Hidden Forest Pond	64
Prajna – The Path to Wisdom	**66**
The Search for Lost Wisdom	67
The Echo of the Silent Mountains	70
The Wise Butterfly	73
Self Respect: The Often Overlooked Value	**76**
The Dancing Butterfly	77
The Song of the Lotus	79
Self Love: Embracing Your True Self	**81**
The Mirror of the Sacred Tree	82
The Song of the Mountains	84
The Riddle of the Peacock	86
Mindfulness: Living in the Here and Now	**88**
The Butterfly's Echo	89
The Riddle of the Still Lake	91
The Cuckoo's Song	93
Positive Thinking: The Power of Thought	**96**
The Stone of Light	97
The Sunflower of Bodhgaya	99
The Lion in the Moonlit Night	101
Non-Self (Anatta): Exploring the True Nature of Our Being	**104**
The Lake's Reflection	105
The Puzzle of the Bamboo Forest	107
The Riddle of the Golden Mirror	109

Equanimity (Upekkha)	**112**
The Valley of Echoes	113
The Queen of the Desert	115
The Dancing Peacock and the Silent Bamboo	117
Rebirth and Karma	**120**
The Song of the Waves	121
The Dance of the Butterfly	124
The Vessel of the Past	126
Suffering and Its Overcoming (Dukkha)	**128**
The Fleeting Paradise	129
The Dance of Shadows	131
The Labyrinth of Emotions	133
Impermanence (Anicca)	**136**
The Crystal Bloom of Anapura	137
The Fading Colors of Mandara	139
The Hourglass Village	141
Afterword and Reflection	**144**
Imprint	**146**

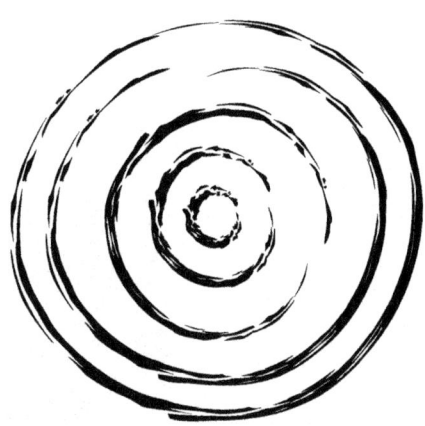

FOREWORD

In quiet moments, when the noise of daily life fades and we find a moment to pause, we often ask ourselves about the meaning, purpose, and sense of our lives.

In such times, we look for guidance, for a light to show us the way and fill us with wisdom. For centuries, the stories and teachings of Buddhism have provided exactly this kind of guidance to many people around the world.

This book is not only a collection of inspiring Buddhist short stories but also a compass for the soul. Each story, each chapter, has been carefully chosen to bring the timeless wisdom of Buddhism into the context of our modern world.

Although Buddhism is deeply rooted in the ancient culture and philosophy of Asia, its messages are universal and timeless. Topics like happiness, inner peace, self-love, and mindfulness are not just relevant to monks in remote monasteries but also to all of us living in today's busy and often overwhelming world.

You don't need to be a Buddhist or follow any religion to appreciate and benefit from the wisdom shared here. The only thing you need is an open heart and an open mind. I invite you to read each story with curiosity and openness, reflect on the lessons within, and use them as guides on your own path to enlightenment.

May these pages bring you peace, clarity, and enlightenment.

INTRODUCTION

THE WHEEL OF DHARMA

Among the many religious and spiritual paths, Buddhism holds a special place for its deep understanding of human nature and its universal teachings of compassion and understanding. At the heart of Buddhism lies the concept of Dharma – a term that means teaching, truth, and law. The Wheel of Dharma symbolizes the core principles and path of Buddhism.

The Dharma Wheel (Dharmachakra)

The Dharmachakra, often shown as a wheel with eight spokes, is a powerful symbol in Buddhism. Each spoke represents one part of the Noble Eightfold Path – the central teaching of the Buddha to end suffering and achieve enlightenment.

The Four Noble Truths

Before exploring the Eightfold Path, we must first understand the Four Noble Truths. These truths are the foundation of Buddhist teaching:

The Truth of Suffering (Dukkha)

Life is impermanent and constantly changing. Clinging to impermanent things causes suffering.

The Truth of the Cause of Suffering (Samudaya)

Ignorance and desire are the main causes of suffering.

The Truth of the End of Suffering (Nirodha)

It is possible to end suffering by overcoming ignorance and desire.

The Truth of the Path that Leads to the End of Suffering (Magga)

This is the Noble Eightfold Path.

The Noble Eightfold Path

Right View (Samma-ditthi)

Understanding reality and the nature of suffering.

Right Intention (Samma-sankappa)

A commitment to ending suffering and practicing compassion and non-harm.

Right Speech (Samma-vaca)

Speaking truthfully and avoiding words that cause harm.

Right Action (Samma-kammanta)

Living ethically and avoiding harmful actions.

Right Livelihood (Samma-ajiva)

Choosing a profession that does no harm and aligns with Buddhist principles.

Right Effort (Samma-vayama)

Working to avoid harmful thoughts and actions while cultivating positive qualities.

Right Mindfulness (Samma-sati)

Developing awareness of your thoughts, feelings, and actions.

Right Concentration (Samma-samadhi)

Focusing and refining the mind through meditation.

The Wheel of Dharma is not just a theoretical guide; it is a living path of transformation. It invites everyone to reflect on their experiences and understanding, leading to deeper awareness and, ultimately, enlightenment.

The principles of the Dharma Wheel are not limited to monks and nuns. They are open to anyone who seeks to live a life of harmony, wisdom, and compassion. It is Buddhism's universal gift to the world – an invitation to lift both heart and mind and to end suffering through deep insight and loving action.

HAPPINESS

IN SEARCH OF TRUE CONTENTMENT

Happiness – that elusive feeling, often like a fleeting shadow – is seen by many as the ultimate goal in life. But what exactly is happiness? Is it something we achieve externally, or is it an inner state? Buddhism teaches us that true happiness is not found in external circumstances or material possessions. It is an inner attitude, a state of mind that comes from deep understanding and acceptance of life.

In the stories that follow, we will look through the lens of wisdom and explore tales from the jungle and beyond to uncover the true nature of happiness. Let us embark on a journey together to discover the many facets of happiness and learn how it can be achieved, no matter the external conditions. May these stories brighten your heart and guide you toward a deeper, lasting happiness.

THE SECRET OF THE LAUGHING TIGER

Deep in the jungle, in a vast, untouched valley, lived a tiger named Raya. Raya was no ordinary tiger. While most tigers were majestic and intimidating, Raya was always cheerful and full of joy. His laughter often echoed through the jungle, and animals from far and wide came to witness this unusual phenomenon.

Raya seemed to be the happiest creature in the jungle, and this fascinated the other animals. Many wondered, "How can a tiger, a predator constantly fighting for survival, be so happy?"

One day, Bala, the oldest and wisest elephant in the jungle, decided to visit Raya to uncover the secret of his happiness.

"Raya," Bala asked, "we all admire you. In the midst of the dangers of the jungle, where life is so uncertain, how can you be so cheerful and happy?"

Raya looked deeply into Bala's eyes and said, "The secret to my happiness, dear Bala, doesn't lie in what I have or don't have. It lies in my attitude and how I see the world."

Bala was puzzled and asked for a clearer explanation.

Raya replied, "Every morning when I wake up, I am grateful for another day in the jungle—for the feel of the grass beneath my paws and the smell of the fresh air. When I hunt, I do so not out of hatred or greed, but out of necessity to survive. I recognize the cycle of life and accept it. If I am unsuccessful, I don't get angry. I trust that the universe will provide for me."

"The true secret of happiness," Raya continued, "is not found in external circumstances but in inner acceptance and trust in life. When we focus on the positive and learn to be present in every moment, we can find happiness even in the hardest times."

Bala was deeply moved by Raya's words. He understood that true happiness does not depend on external conditions but on one's inner mindset and perspective.

From that day forward, the message of the laughing tiger spread throughout the jungle. Many animals began to change their outlook and find joy in the small things in life.

And so, the secret of happiness, once the mystery of the laughing tiger, became the wisdom of the entire jungle.

MEANING & LESSON

This story reminds us that true happiness often lies hidden in the simplest moments of life and is not always found in grand or obvious things. Instead of constantly chasing external success or recognition, we should learn to appreciate the joy of the present and find happiness in the little things.

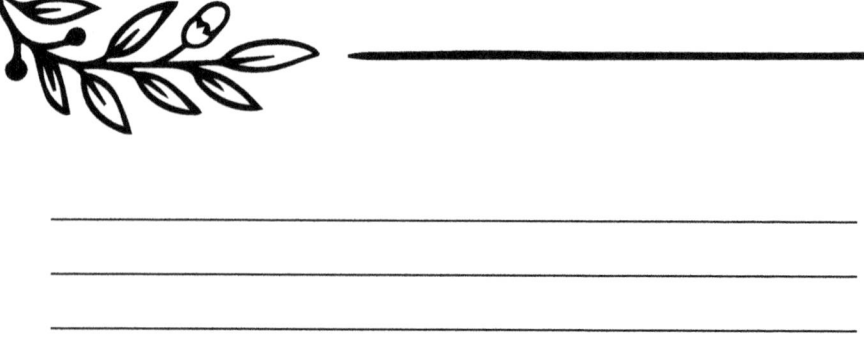

SELF-REFLECTION

What joys and moments of happiness in your life might you be overlooking as you constantly search for something bigger or better, much like the animals in the jungle who didn't understand the tiger's laughter? How can you learn to value happiness in the simple and present moments?

_____

_____

_____

THE SONG OF THE SILENT STREAM

In a remote village, surrounded by towering mountains and dense forests, a small, clear stream flowed. The villagers took the stream for granted, paying it little attention. But an old monk, who lived nearby, spent hours every day by the stream, listening to its gentle murmur and meditating.

One day, a traveler came to the village. He had heard of the old monk's wisdom and sought his advice. "Revered monk," he asked, "I have traveled through many lands in search of the secret to happiness. I have gathered riches, gained fame, and achieved everything one could desire. Yet deep inside, I feel an emptiness. What am I missing?"

The monk opened his eyes, smiled, and pointed to the stream. "Have you heard the song of this stream?" he asked.
The traveler was puzzled. "It's just an ordinary stream, trickling. What's so special about it?"

The monk replied, "This stream has taught me the true secret of happiness. It flows constantly, never stopping or complaining, no matter what obstacles lie in its path. It clings to nothing and holds on to nothing. Yet it always sings a song of joy and peace."

The monk continued, "The secret of happiness is not in possessing or achieving things but in the ability to be in the here and now, without attachment or resistance. Just as this stream flows freely and clings to nothing, we too must learn to accept life as it comes and find joy and peace in each moment."

The traveler was deeply moved by the monk's words. He realized that true happiness does not depend on external conditions but on one's inner attitude and acceptance of the present moment.

From that day forward, he abandoned his search for external happiness and began to carry the song of the silent stream in his heart. Though outwardly he remained the same traveler, those who met him could feel a deep calm and joy radiating from within.

MEANING & LESSON

This story reminds us that true happiness is often found in subtle, quiet moments that are easy to overlook. It encourages us to pause, listen, and appreciate the often unnoticed sources of joy around us.

SELF-REFLECTION

"How often do you miss the gentle melodies of happiness in your life because you are too busy or distracted by the loud noises of the world?"

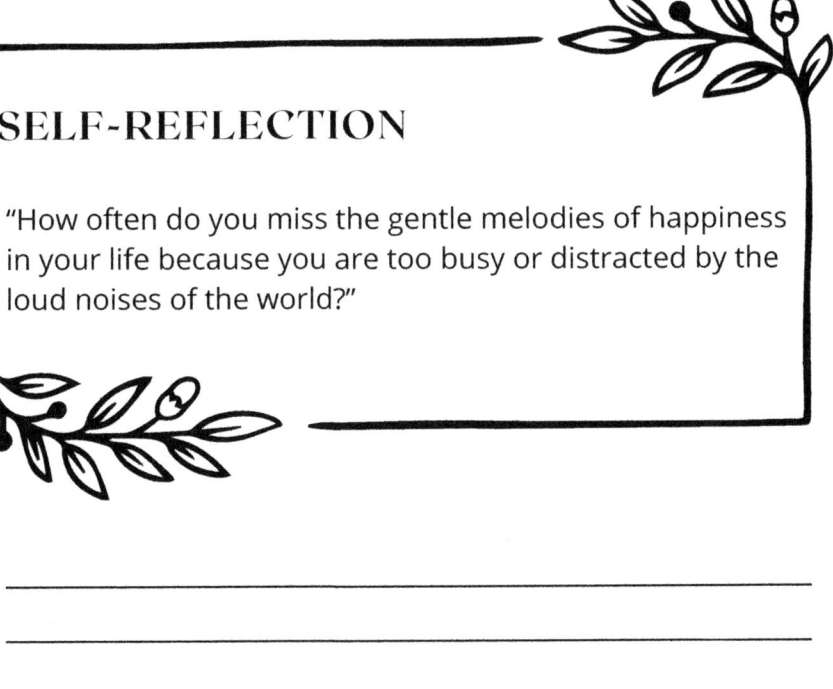

_____
_____
_____

THE DANCE OF THE WIND

In the endless plains of a barren desert, where life was sparse and the sky stretched endlessly, there existed a powerful, vibrant wind known as "Anila." Anila was no ordinary wind; he was renowned for his ability to shape sand dunes, erase old trails, and create new paths.

Yet, despite his power, Anila often felt lonely. He gazed at the steadfast mountains in the distance and envied their permanence, while he himself was shapeless and fleeting.

One day, as Anila sang his melody of melancholy, he heard a gentle voice. It was Mara, the old cactus, who had stood in the desert for centuries. "Why do you sing a song of sadness, mighty wind?" Mara asked.

Anila replied, "I have no form, no fixed place to belong. I am always moving, while you and the mountains stand firm and watch the world around you. I envy your steadiness."

Mara chuckled softly. "You don't understand, Anila. It is your freedom and unbounded nature that make you unique. While I am rooted here and the mountains cannot move, you have the freedom to explore the whole world, discover new places, and experience life from countless perspectives."

Anila pondered this and asked, "But what about happiness? Where can I find it?"

Mara replied: "Happiness doesn't lie in stillness or motion, in having or not having. It lies in accepting what is. You are the wind, powerful and free. Find joy in your nature, in your dance through the desert and the sky."

From that moment, Anila no longer saw the desert as a place of loneliness but as his stage—a place where he could dance, sing, and express himself. He found delight in shaping the dunes, playing with the birds, and sharing the stories of the desert.

And so, in the vastness of the desert, Anila danced and sang his new song of happiness, and all the creatures, whether rooted or fleeting, celebrated the joy of being.

MEANING & LESSON

The story highlights the importance of freeing ourselves from rigid expectations and allowing the spontaneous and unpredictable moments of happiness to guide us. It teaches us to embrace life in all its forms and be inspired by the simple joy of being.

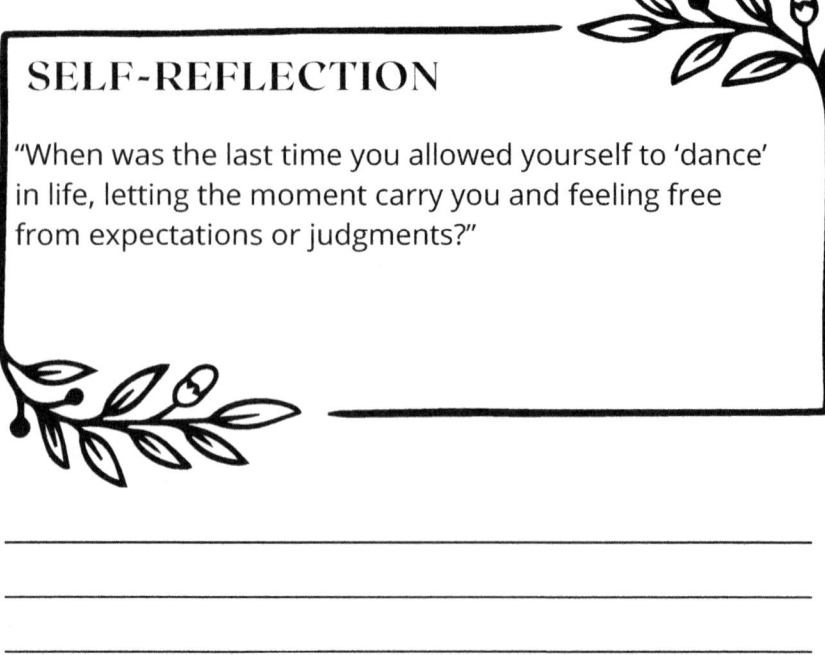

SELF-REFLECTION

"When was the last time you allowed yourself to 'dance' in life, letting the moment carry you and feeling free from expectations or judgments?"

_____
_____
_____

"There is no path to happiness—happiness is the path."

— GAUTAMA BUDDHA

INNER PEACE

THE SILENT LAKE WITHIN

Inner Peace, a state of calm and serenity, inner peace can be elusive in a world full of turmoil, distractions, and constant change. Yet it is precisely within this complex and ever-shifting landscape that the key to discovering this profound sense of stillness and harmony lies—waiting within each of us. Buddhism teaches that inner peace is not something gained from external sources but rather an inward journey, a deep dive into one's own being to quiet the constant chatter of the mind and find a space of stillness and tranquility.

The following Buddhist short stories serve as a guide and inspiration for this journey. They offer not only the wisdom of ancient masters but also practical lessons to help overcome the noise of the world and discover the sweet melody of inner peace. Let these tales lead you into a state of reflection and meditation, and guide you to the silent, peaceful place within your heart. May each story serve as a step on your path to inner harmony.

THE ENCHANTED TEMPLE RUIN

In a remote village, surrounded by towering mountains and dense forests, there stood an ancient temple abandoned for generations. The villagers avoided the place, as rumors spoke of a ghost that haunted the temple, bringing unbearable noise to anyone who ventured near.

One day, a wandering monk arrived in the village. Upon hearing of the abandoned temple, he decided to spend the night there. The villagers urgently warned him about the ghost, but the monk only smiled gently and made his way to the temple.

As the monk entered the temple, he was greeted by a deafening noise. The air was filled with the sound of clanging bells, howling winds, and screaming animals. But instead of fleeing, the monk sat down in meditation and focused on his breath.

Hours passed, and the monk remained steady and calm. At last, as the first ray of morning sunlight touched the temple floor, the noise ceased. In its place, a profound silence spread, deeper than any quiet the monk had ever known.

The monk opened his eyes and saw an old spirit standing before him. "Why did you not flee?" the spirit asked.

The monk replied, "The noise outside us can only have power over us if we allow it to echo within. I sought the stillness within myself, and in that stillness, your noise lost its power."

The spirit, visibly moved, said, "For centuries, I have sought someone to show me this path to inner stillness. Thanks to you, I have now found it." With these words, the spirit vanished, and the temple became a place of peace and meditation.

The villagers were astonished to see the monk emerge unscathed from the temple the next morning. From that day on, the temple became a center of learning and meditation, where many discovered the path to inner peace.

MEANING & LESSON

This story reminds us that true inner peace does not depend on external circumstances but on our ability to find and preserve stillness within ourselves.

SELF-REFLECTION

"In what areas of your life do you see only ruins and decay, without recognizing the hidden potential or concealed beauty? How might you change your perspective to discover the 'enchanted' within the seeming 'ruins' of your life?"

_____
_____
_____

THE MONKEY AND THE QUIET LAKE

In the dense jungles of Banyan, far from human villages, lived Miko, a young and lively monkey. Miko was known for his constant restlessness and mischief. He jumped from branch to branch, disturbed other animals, and simply couldn't sit still. His energy was infectious but often overwhelming for the other jungle creatures.

One day, while frolicking through the jungle, he discovered a clear, silent lake. The surface of the lake was so calm that it perfectly reflected the sky. From a nearby tree, Miko watched the lake, captivated by its stillness. He had never seen anything like it before.

Cautiously, he approached the lake and threw a stone into it. The tranquil surface rippled, shattering the sky's reflection into a thousand pieces. Yet after a while, the lake returned to its original calm.

Miko was amazed. Each time he disturbed the lake, it always returned to its peaceful state. Day after day, Miko returned to the lake and observed its calm surface. He began meditating, focusing on the quiet lake and trying to find that inner stillness within himself.

Months passed, and the once restless monkey grew calmer and more composed. The other animals noticed the change and grew curious. Miko led them to the lake and shared the lessons he had learned. "When we recognize and accept our inner restlessness," he explained, "we can return to a state of inner peace, just as this lake does after being disturbed."

The jungle animals began to view the lake as a sacred place of meditation, and many found their own inner peace there.

Miko's transformation became a legend in the jungles of Banyan. The silent lake served as a reminder that amidst the chaos and turmoil of life, there is always a space for inner peace—we just need to find it and protect it.

MEANING & LESSON

This story teaches us that inner peace does not depend on how calm our surroundings are but on how calm we are within ourselves. It is possible to find serenity and composure even in the most turbulent times.

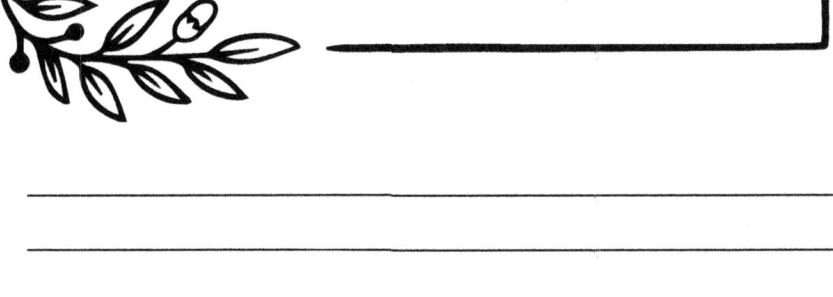

SELF-REFLECTION

"In what moments of your life have you, like the monkey, been swept away by external distractions and chaos instead of resting in the stillness of your own inner lake? How can you be more mindful in the future about maintaining your inner balance and tranquility?"

_____
_____
_____

THE WHITE STONE OF PEACE

Deep in the valleys of the Anapura mountain range, surrounded by dense forests and rushing rivers, there lay a remarkable stone. This stone was unlike any other. It was large and spherical, with a smooth, shimmering surface. The locals called it "Pax," which in their language meant "peace."

Over time, many legends grew around Pax. It was said to be thousands of years old and to have witnessed countless wars, storms, and disasters. Yet, while the world around it fell into chaos and turmoil, Pax remained steadfastly calm and still.

Travelers from distant lands came to see Pax and feel its tranquil presence. It was said that anyone who placed their hand on Pax and took a deep breath would experience a moment of absolute inner peace. Despite the storms of life, the fears, and worries that people carried, Pax remained serene and untouched.

A powerful king heard of Pax and decided to bring the stone to his palace. He believed that if he owned Pax, eternal peace would come to his kingdom. But when he tried to move the stone, it wouldn't budge. No army, no machine, nothing could dislodge Pax from its place. Enraged, the king ordered the stone to be broken, but the tools shattered, and Pax remained unscathed.

In his frustration, the king summoned a wise elder and asked him about the secret of Pax. The elder smiled and said, "Pax is not just a stone. It is a symbol of inner peace, which cannot be shaken by external forces. Inner peace cannot be owned, controlled, or destroyed. It can only be experienced."

The king understood and left Pax alone. He often returned to the valley to meditate before the stone and find his own inner peace.

MEANING & LESSON

The legend of Pax teaches us that true inner peace does not depend on external circumstances. It is always within us, ready to be discovered, no matter the storms raging around us. Inner peace is not determined by our surroundings but by the stillness we cultivate within ourselves. Even in the most turbulent times, it is possible to find calm and serenity.

SELF-REFLECTION

What are the 'external forces' in your life that you believe disrupt your inner peace, and how can you, like the stone Pax, remain steadfast in your inner calm despite the turbulence around you?

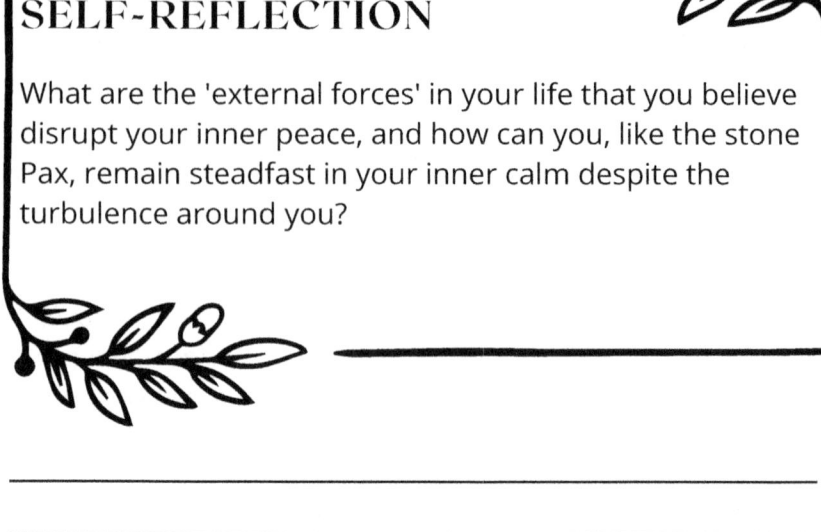

_____
_____
_____

"Peace comes from within. Do not seek it outside."

– GAUTAMA BUDDHA

SELF-ACCEPTANCE

THE FIRST STEP TO LIBERATION

Self-acceptance is a fundamental part of inner peace and well-being. In a world that constantly strives to be the best, the biggest, and the most beautiful, we often forget to accept ourselves just as we are. Buddhist teachings remind us that all suffering arises from ignorance and attachment—and that recognizing our true nature is the key to freeing ourselves from this suffering. Through the following stories about self-acceptance, we hope readers will feel a deeper connection to their authentic selves and discover the freedom that unfolds when we fully embrace and love what is.

THE FLOWER AMIDST THE STONES

In an ancient temple surrounded by rocky paths, a solitary flower grew through a crack in the stones. Each day, it was admired by the monks and pilgrims who visited the temple.

"How can such a beautiful flower grow in such an inhospitable place?" a young monk asked his teacher.

The old master smiled and said, "The flower did not seek out a perfect spot to grow. It simply accepted the place life gave it and decided to bloom there."

Months went by, and the flower kept on blooming, braving wind and weather, and radiating its full splendor among the hard stones.

One day, the master said to the young monk, "Just like this flower, you must learn to accept yourself. It doesn't matter where you are or what circumstances you live in. True self-acceptance means realizing that you can bloom right where you are."

The young monk understood and began to appreciate both himself and his surroundings more deeply. He realized that self-acceptance does not mean settling for less, but rather recognizing that true beauty and strength come from within—not from external conditions.

MEANING & LESSON

"The Flower Amidst the Stones" teaches us that true self-acceptance does not depend on external conditions, but rather on our inner attitude toward ourselves and our circumstances. It's about recognizing that we can bloom anywhere, under any conditions, when we accept ourselves and acknowledge our own strength and beauty.

SELF-REFLECTION

In which areas of your life do you feel like the flower growing among the stones, and how could you use these circumstances as an opportunity to flourish in your own unique way?

_____

_____

_____

THE UNADORNED MIRROR

In a distant kingdom at the edge of the Himalayas stood a temple renowned for its remarkable golden mirror. Pilgrims from all corners of the land traveled there to gaze upon it. It was said that anyone who looked into this mirror would see their true nature—without ornament, without illusion, untouched by the world outside.

A young monk named Arav heard of this mirror and set out on a journey to behold his truest self. Months went by, and after many trials, he finally stood before the golden mirror. Yet when he looked inside, he saw only a young man, exactly as he was, with no extraordinary features or signs of divine insight.

Disappointed, Arav asked the temple guardian, "I heard about a mirror that reveals one's true self. But all I see is just me, as I am. Where is the secret I've been seeking?"

Smiling, the guardian replied, "Young monk, the mirror shows that there are no embellishments or illusions you must cast off. You are already perfect in your own uniqueness. The secret lies in accepting yourself just as you are, without feeling the need for change or validation."

Arav understood. He returned to his monastery with a peaceful heart, having realized the value of self-acceptance. There, he taught others to cherish the unadorned mirror of their own souls.

MEANING & LESSON

"The Unadorned Mirror" reminds us of the importance of self-acceptance. True insight does not come from chasing external shine or recognition but from recognizing and appreciating our own inner completeness. The greatest gift we can give ourselves is to acknowledge and value our true self.

SELF-REFLECTION

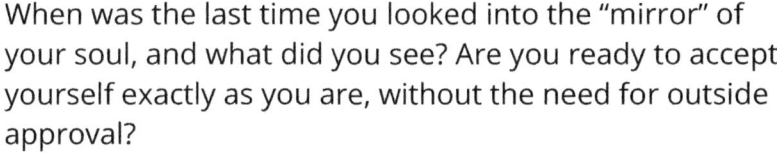

When was the last time you looked into the "mirror" of your soul, and what did you see? Are you ready to accept yourself exactly as you are, without the need for outside approval?

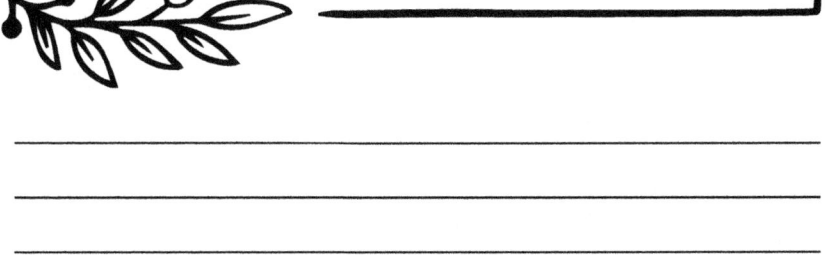

_____
_____
_____

THE GARDEN OF THE SELF

In a small village at the foot of the mountains, there was a garden renowned for its incomparable beauty. It bloomed all year round, filled with vibrant colors, fragrances, and sounds. But the most astonishing thing about this garden was that it had no gardener.

The villagers wondered how a garden could flourish so magnificently without anyone tending to it. An old wise woman named Devika, who lived on the outskirts of the village, knew the garden's secret. One day, the villagers asked her about the mystery behind the garden in perpetual bloom.

Devika smiled and said, "This garden is a reflection of our inner self. Every plant, every stone, and every drop of water represents a part of us—our strengths, our weaknesses, our hopes, and our fears. The garden needs no gardener because it accepts itself just as it is. It does not fight the weeds or wish for more flowers; it simply exists in its own wholeness."

The villagers were amazed. Some began visiting the garden in meditation, while others reflected on what it meant to accept themselves exactly as they are.

MEANING & LESSON

"The Garden of the Self" shows that true beauty and harmony arise from complete self-acceptance. There is no need to constantly force change or improvement upon ourselves; genuine happiness and peace come from embracing and appreciating every aspect of who we are, both light and dark. It teaches us to view ourselves through the lens of acceptance and to realize that we are already whole.

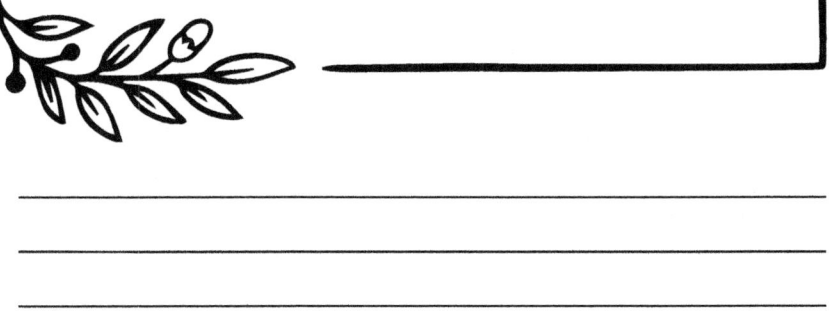

SELF-REFLECTION

If your inner self were a garden, what would it look like? Which parts of your garden have you overlooked or failed to embrace until now?

_____
_____
_____

COMPASSION

At the heart of Buddhism and Hinduism lies a powerful concept of compassion known as "Karuna." Compassion is not merely a feeling of pity for the suffering of others, but also the ardent desire to alleviate that suffering. It is the profound understanding of the interconnectedness of all living beings—the recognition that one person's pain is shared by all.

Karuna encourages us to look beyond our own ego and see the world through the eyes of the heart. In the following stories, we will explore the many facets of Karuna and discover how genuine compassion can transform our lives and the lives of those around us. You will encounter ancient sages, brave heroes, and ordinary people—all bound by this mighty thread of compassion. May their stories inspire you and guide you in acting with a heart full of compassion in every situation.

THE MONK'S SONG

In a remote village at the foot of the Himalayas lived a young monk named Aravind. Each morning, he went to the village well to draw water, and every time he noticed an old man named Hari, sitting there for hours, staring sadly into the distance. Hari was known as the "Silent Elder," for he had not spoken a word in decades.

One day, as Aravind fetched water, he sat beside Hari and asked, "Why do you sit here every day, gazing so mournfully into the distance?" Hari did not respond, but a tear rolled down his cheek.

Aravind realized that words alone might not reach Hari. So, he took out his flute and began to play a gentle melody. The tune was so sweet and wistful that even the birds fell silent to listen. When the last note had faded, Aravind saw that Hari's eyes were no longer dull—they were brimming with tears.

Slowly, Hari opened his mouth and spoke: "That song reminds me of my wife, who passed away many years ago. We often sat here by the well, watching the stars together."

Aravind smiled and said, "Music has the power to touch our deepest emotions. I hope this song has brought you a bit of comfort." Hari nodded and smiled for the first time in years.

From that day on, Aravind played his flute each morning for Hari and for anyone else in the village who needed solace or compassion.

The tune became known as "The Monk's Song" and spread to neighboring villages.

People from all around began to come and listen, sharing their sorrows and fears. In time, Aravind was known not only as a gifted flute player but also as someone who showed true compassion through his music.

MEANING & LESSON

"The Monk's Song" illustrates that genuine compassion often goes beyond merely listening or understanding. Sometimes, it is the simple gestures—like a song, a smile, or a silent embrace—that can ease the deepest pain. Recognizing another's suffering and acting on it, even in the most modest way, lies at the heart of true compassion.

SELF-REFLECTION

In which moments of our lives could we pause, truly listen, and show compassion—even when no words are spoken?

_____

_____

THE ELEPHANT'S TEARS

Deep in the forests of India lived a mighty elephant named Ekalinga. Known for his immense strength and stature, he commanded the respect of all the animals around him. Yet despite his power, Ekalinga was a gentle soul who showed extraordinary compassion.

In the same region lived a clever rabbit named Mira, who often found herself in tricky situations. One day, Mira fell into a deep pit that hunters had dug to trap wild animals. She called for help, but none of the other animals dared come near the pit, afraid they too would be captured.

Ekalinga heard Mira's cries and hurried to the pit. He extended his trunk to rescue her, but the sides were too steep and slippery. In despair, Mira began to cry—and to her surprise, Ekalinga also started to shed tears, which fell into the pit and gradually filled it with water.

When the water rose high enough, Mira was able to climb onto a nearby rock and finally escape. All the forest creatures were astonished by the miracle they had witnessed.

"Why were you crying, Ekalinga?" Mira asked. The great elephant replied, "Your pain ran so deep that I could feel it in my own heart. My tears were not from sadness, but from compassion."

From that day on, the tale of Ekalinga's compassionate tears spread throughout the forest. All the animals came to understand that true strength does not lie in physical might, but in the capacity to feel and show compassion toward others.

MEANING & LESSON

"The Elephant's Tears" reminds us that compassion is a universal emotion present in all beings, great or small. True greatness is not defined by physical power but by the ability to empathize and extend compassion to others.

SELF-REFLECTION

How often do we allow our hearts to be moved by another's pain, and how often do we respond with genuine compassion in times of need?

_____

_____

_____

THE PETRIFIED GARDEN

In a secluded part of the Himalayas lay a most unusual place known as the "Petrified Garden." Every plant, every animal, and even the birds in flight had turned to stone. Despite its haunting beauty, few ventured there because of a legend that anyone who entered would likewise be turned to stone.

A Buddhist monk named Wimal heard of this garden and decided to visit. Upon entering, he discovered at its center a large statue of a weeping woman. Sensing that this statue held the key to the garden's secret, he sat beside it and entered deep meditation.

In his meditation, Wimal saw the woman as she once was: a kindhearted gardener named Laya, who had lovingly tended the garden. She was so deeply connected to every living thing there that she took on all their pain and suffering. Her compassion overwhelmed her; she bore the garden's sorrow within herself, and on the day she wept, the entire garden became locked in stone, trapped by her indescribable grief.

Wimal realized that although Laya's compassion was profound, it lacked the wisdom to let go and accept the natural flow of life. He began to chant a mantra of compassion, restoring balance between love and release in Laya's heart.

Slowly, the petrified plants and animals came back to life. Laya herself emerged from her stone form and stood before Wimal, alive again.

Grateful, she said, "I was imprisoned by my own love and compassion, not understanding that true compassion also means letting go."

Wimal nodded. "Compassion without wisdom can bind us," he said, "but together, they can work miracles."

MEANING & LESSON

"The Petrified Garden" teaches us that while compassion is a noble virtue, without the wisdom to let go, it can hold us captive. True compassion requires not only love but also the understanding that sometimes the best we can do is to release our hold and allow the universe to take its course.

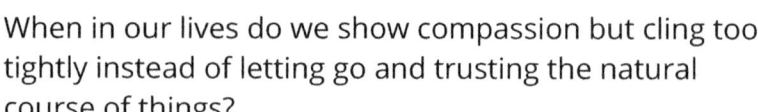

SELF-REFLECTION

When in our lives do we show compassion but cling too tightly instead of letting go and trusting the natural course of things?

"Compassion is the wish for all beings to be free from suffering."

– BHAGAVAD GITA

"When someone sees all beings within the Self and the Self within all beings, they harbor hatred toward none."

– DALAI LAMA

KINDNESS

METTA

Within the profound wisdom of Buddhist and Hindu traditions, "Metta"—often translated as "loving-kindness"—is a central concept. It is not merely an emotion but a heartfelt attitude, a state of being. Metta is the sincere wish and intention that all beings, without exception, be truly happy and free from suffering. It is a universal, unconditional, and selfless desire for the well-being and joy of all.

In a world often marked by conflict, misunderstandings, and isolation, Metta offers a path of healing, understanding, and deeper human connection. By turning to stories about Metta, we do more than immerse ourselves in inspiring narratives; we learn how to anchor this powerful principle in our own lives.

THE SONG OF THE FORGOTTEN GARDEN

In a far-off kingdom, surrounded by towering mountains and dense forests, lay a village whose centerpiece was an ancient temple once graced by a magnificent garden. In earlier times, this garden was alive with vibrant flowers in full bloom, and its clear streams sparkled and flowed freely. But now, it was barren and cracked—dry and lifeless. The elders said a curse had befallen the garden, and as the years passed, the villagers avoided this once-sacred place.

A wanderer, traveling from a distant land in search of wisdom, arrived in the village. Upon hearing of the cursed garden, he felt inexplicably drawn to it. At the center of the garden, he discovered—much to his surprise—a solitary flower blooming defiantly among the cracks. It seemed to be the last remnant of the garden's former glory.

Each morning at sunrise and each evening as the sun sank behind the mountains, the wanderer visited the garden. He sang ancient songs, told stories, and gently poured water onto the parched ground. From a distance, the villagers watched and smiled at what they believed to be his futile efforts.

Yet, after a few weeks, the garden began to change. Delicate blades of grass emerged from the once-dry soil, flowers blossomed here and there, and the air filled with the scent of spring. The villagers ventured closer and joined the wanderer in restoring the garden.

Before long, water once again flowed in the streams, birds returned to sing their songs, and the garden shone with renewed splendor.

When the wanderer continued on his journey, he left behind a village that had rediscovered not only a garden but also its belief in the transformative power of kindness.

MEANING & LESSON

"The Song of the Forgotten Garden" reminds us that with persistence, love, and dedication, even the most forsaken places can be revived. It teaches us that kindness and endurance are often the keys to bringing about change and restoring lost beauty.

SELF-REFLECTION

Where in your life could you "sing songs" and "pour water" with patience and perseverance to transform desolation into hope?

_____

_____

THE ANIMALS' FEAST IN THE VALLEY OF DHARA

In a secluded valley called Dhara, surrounded by the majestic peaks of the Himalayas, many animals lived in an idyllic setting. For centuries, the valley had provided everything the creatures needed: lush grass, crystal-clear water, and trees laden with succulent fruit. But one year, after an unusually brief monsoon, the rains did not return. The once-babbling streams ran dry, and green turned to brown.

In these challenging times, a wise and elderly porcupine—revered as Guru Bhara—had an idea. He proposed hosting a grand feast for all the animals of the valley. The plan was simple: every creature, regardless of size or status, would contribute something to the feast. Some animals were hesitant—especially the fox, who wondered what he could possibly offer in such a barren season.

But the birds sang songs to spread word of the feast. The beaver, known for his building skills, constructed a vast platform using wood and leaves. The butterflies adorned the area with colorful flowers. Even the temperamental fox brought out some hidden fruit reserves he had stored away.

When the feast began, the valley witnessed scenes never before seen: a tiger sharing his meal with a deer, an elephant laughing with a squirrel, and a wolf dancing with a hare. It was a celebration of unity, sharing, and joy.

Yet the greatest wonder happened after the feast. Animals that had once formed separate groups began working together to find water sources. The fox, with his keen sense of smell, located a hidden spring he had once intended to keep secret for himself. And the elephant, with his tremendous strength, helped dig out the ground so that all could drink.

Dhara Valley returned to its former glory, but something had changed. It was not only the physical water that brought the animals together—it was the kindness and compassion they had displayed during the feast. That was the true source of their abundance.

MEANING & LESSON

"The Animals' Feast in the Valley of Dhara" shows us that true kindness and generosity often emerge most vividly in challenging times. It also illustrates that coming together and sharing is more than a physical act—it is a spiritual one that places the well-being of the community above individual needs.

SELF-REFLECTION

At which moments in your life have you felt the power of community and compassion most strongly?

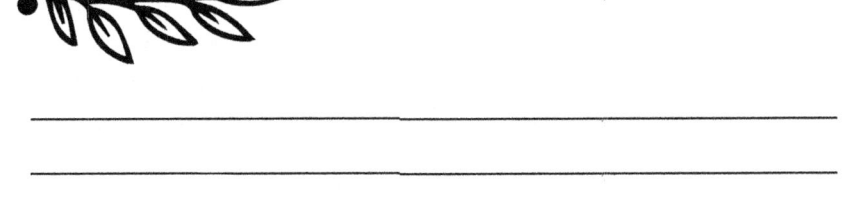

_____
_____
_____

THE SINGING BAMBOO GROVE

At the foot of the Himalayas lay a small village beside a dense bamboo grove renowned for a unique characteristic. When the wind blew through the grove, the bamboo stalks produced harmonious melodies, as if they were a chorus of celestial voices. Pilgrims from all over traveled to experience this phenomenon and meditate in the grove's tranquility.

One day, a young monk named Deva arrived in the village. He sought answers to his spiritual questions and hoped to find enlightenment in the singing bamboo grove. To his surprise, however, he discovered that some of the bamboo stalks did not sing at all. They stood still and silent while the others produced their melodic sounds.

Puzzled, Deva asked the villagers why certain bamboo did not sing. An elderly woman named Tara explained, "Those silent bamboo stalks never received any kindness. A bamboo does not sing of its own accord. It sings because it was nurtured and sustained by others. Anyone who watered and cared for it in its youth gave it the ability to sing."

Deva understood. He spent the following weeks tending to the silent bamboo, watering and caring for them, speaking and even singing to them. In time, they too began to sing—tentatively at first, but growing stronger each day, eventually harmonizing with the rest of the grove.

When Deva departed the village, he left behind not only a fully singing bamboo grove but also a lesson for the villagers and for all who came to witness the phenomenon: kindness is like water that nourishes the heart and allows it to reveal its true melody.

MEANING & LESSON

"The Singing Bamboo Grove" illustrates that through kindness and care, we can spark change both outwardly and within. It reminds us that all beings—whether human, animal, or plant—can flourish and realize their true potential through acts of kindness.

SELF-REFLECTION

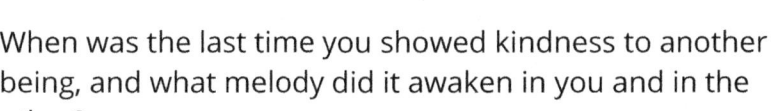

When was the last time you showed kindness to another being, and what melody did it awaken in you and in the other?

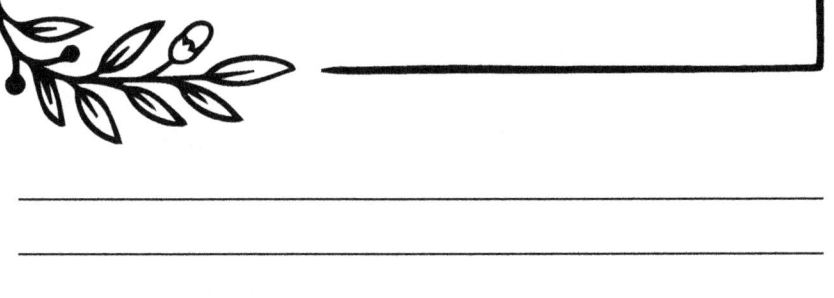

_____
_____
_____

MORALITY AND ETHICS

SILA

Within the profound teachings of Buddhism and Hinduism, "sila" or morality and ethics forms the bedrock of any spiritual path. These are not merely rules to be followed, but guiding principles that help us live in harmony with both the world around us and our own inner being. They teach us to conduct our lives so that our actions serve not only our own welfare but also that of all living beings. Viewed in a universal context, "sila" is seen as a means to create balance between our individual existence and the universal whole. It serves as a bridge between the individual self and the collective. Before we dive into the inspiring stories on morality and ethics, it's important to remember that true "sila" comes from within—never imposed by external force. It is an inner compass that guides us when navigating life's turbulent waters.

THE UNSEEDED FIELD

In a remote village at the foot of the Himalayas, there was a large, fertile field that, strangely, no one had ever cultivated. Despite its potential to produce enough food for the entire village, generations of farmers avoided it. A persistent rumor claimed that anyone who worked the field would suffer immeasurable hardship.

One day, a wise monk arrived in the village and heard about this unseeded field. Curious, he decided to plant crops there himself. Though the villagers warned him, he simply smiled and began his work. He plowed, sowed, and tended the field with utmost care.
Months went by, and to everyone's amazement, the field yielded a rich harvest. The monk distributed all of it among the villagers, then asked them to cultivate the field together in the coming years.

Although skeptical, the villagers were persuaded by the monk's wisdom and kindness. Under his guidance, they cooperated—and year after year, the field prospered. Not once did any of the rumored disasters come to pass.

> Before continuing on his journey, the monk was asked by the villagers why the curse had not harmed him after he tilled the field. Smiling, he replied, "The field was never cursed. It was your fear that prevented you from seeing its potential. Through collaboration and sincere intentions, you have discovered the field's true worth."

MEANING & LESSON

This story illustrates how unfounded fears and rumors can keep us from realizing our full capabilities. By showing courage, working together, and acting with pure intention, we can overcome these barriers and experience genuine abundance.

SELF-REFLECTION

Which unseeded fields in your life are you avoiding out of fear, and how could you uncover their true potential?

THE RIDDLE OF THE SACRED POND

Deep within a dense forest stood a pond considered sacred. Legend claimed that anyone who drank from its waters would gain immeasurable wisdom. Animals from every corner of the forest came to sample its magic. Yet there was always a strict rule: only one animal could drink from the pond at a time.

One day, an elephant and a hare arrived simultaneously. Weary from their journeys and impatient in the face of the pond's promise, each wanted to drink first. The mighty, proud elephant demanded that the hare yield to him. But this time, the hare—who had often been intimidated by larger animals—refused. He argued that genuine wisdom meant respecting even the smallest creatures.

An old crane, who had lived near the pond for many years, observed and suggested a way to resolve the matter: solve the pond's riddle to determine who should drink first. "The pond will reward the animal that truly understands the essence of ethics and morality," he said.

The crane posed a question: "Which is heavier—a basket full of feathers or a heart full of greed?"

Confident in his superiority, the elephant immediately answered, "A basket full of feathers."

The hare, however, paused to think and then replied, "A heart full of greed is heavier because it weighs down the soul."

Nodding, the crane allowed the hare to drink first. Initially ashamed, the elephant soon recognized the hare's wisdom and waited patiently for his turn.

MEANING & LESSON

This story teaches that genuine wisdom often resides in humility and reflection, not in physical power or hasty judgments. It is vital to look inward and understand what truly drives us.

SELF-REFLECTION

What weighs on your heart, and how does it influence your choices and behavior?

_____

_____

_____

THE SONG OF THE JUNGLE

Amid the lush greenery of the jungle stood an ancient banyan tree known as the sage of the forest. Under its wide-reaching branches, animals often gathered for guidance or simply to find shelter.

On a scorching summer day, the jungle's inhabitants congregated beneath the banyan tree, seeking respite from the heat. They began boasting of their feats and prowess: the proud lion spoke of his conquests, the cunning fox of his cleverness, and the mighty elephant of his strength.

Meanwhile, a small bird perched on a low branch quietly sang a gentle, sweet melody that went nearly unnoticed. As the animals' boasting grew louder, the banyan tree asked, "What truly makes you strong and noble in this jungle?"

The creatures fell silent and reflected. The little bird kept singing. After a moment, the banyan tree continued, "Do you hear the bird's song? It is a melody of gratitude and humility. While you celebrate your achievements, it praises the beauty of the jungle and the goodness of nature."

Ashamed of their self-importance, the animals realized that true strength does not lie in dominating others, but in humility and gratitude.

MEANING & LESSON

This story illustrates that real greatness is not found in outward displays of power, but in our capacity for humility and thankfulness. We must learn to appreciate life's simpler wonders and to recognize the beauty and kindness that surrounds us.

SELF-REFLECTION

What is your song, and how does it reflect your values and convictions?

_____
_____
_____

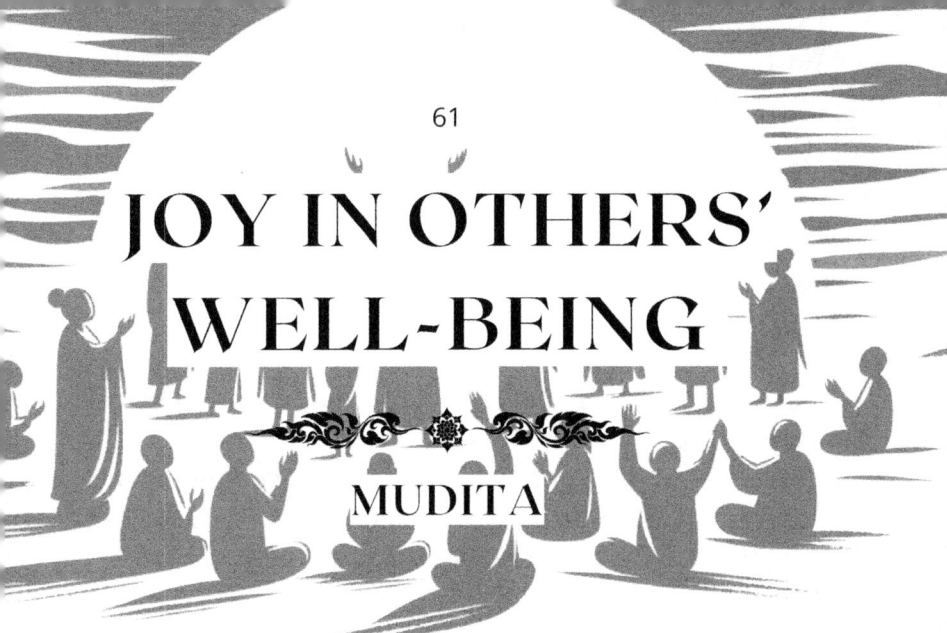

JOY IN OTHERS' WELL-BEING

MUDITA

At the heart of Buddhist and Hindu teachings lies the concept of the interconnectedness of all living beings. One of the most sublime emotions that springs from this unity is the joy we feel in others' well-being, known as Mudita. This is an altruistic happiness found in the success and joy of others—free from envy or jealousy. It is the exact opposite of taking pleasure in another's misfortune and reflects the noblest qualities of the human heart. Mudita reminds us that true happiness is not found only in our own prosperity, but also in celebrating the well-being of others. It challenges us to look beyond ourselves and to recognize—and nurture—the collective joy that binds us all.

In an age often dominated by comparison and competition, Mudita teaches us to build bridges of shared happiness and to embrace the triumphs of others as if they were our own. In the following stories, we will explore the profound meaning of Mudita and the wonderful ways we can cultivate this joyful spirit in everyday life.

THE RIDDLE OF THE TEMPLE PAINTING

In a remote village at the foot of the Himalayas stood an ancient temple, famous for centuries for its mystical mural. The painting depicted a young prince holding a golden orb. Every year, thousands of pilgrims visited the village to view this artwork, yet the story behind it remained unknown.

When the wise monk Harsha heard about this mysterious painting, he decided to see it for himself. The villagers, eager for his insight, led him reverently to the temple. After studying the painting at length, Harsha turned to those gathered and asked, "Tell me, what do you see in this image?"

Their answers varied. Some spoke of the prince's grandeur; others focused on the gleaming orb. After everyone had answered, Harsha smiled and said, "I see a prince who is not clutching the orb, but offering it to the viewer. This image teaches us that true ethics and morality lie not in holding on, but in sharing and giving."

Astonished, the villagers gazed at the painting again. Indeed, it now appeared as if the prince were presenting the orb. Word of this realization swept through the village like wildfire. From then on, people revered the painting not just as a work of art, but also as a symbol of selflessness and caring for others.

Months later, as Harsha continued on his journey, the villagers decided to hold an annual festival in honor of the prince and his message of selflessness.

MEANING & LESSON

This tale highlights the value of sharing and giving beyond mere material possessions. It teaches that genuine ethics and morality are rooted in selflessness and a commitment to the well-being of the community. Ultimately, it encourages us to look beyond our own interests and to cultivate true generosity.

SELF-REFLECTION

When in your life have you experienced or shown true generosity, expecting nothing in return?

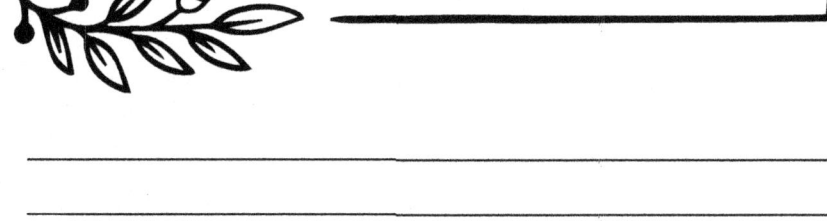

_____

_____

_____

THE HIDDEN FOREST POND

In the heart of an Indian forest, far from busy villages, lay a secret pond. Its waters had a remarkable property: whoever drank from it once would never thirst again. But there was a catch—each creature could only drink once, and never again.

An old sage named Nalaka knew of the pond's secret and guarded it carefully. He feared that many, upon discovering its power, might try to claim it for themselves, misusing the gift of eternal thirst-quenching.

One day, however, a thirst-ridden deer stumbled upon the pond and took a drink. At once, his thirst vanished forever. Overcome with gratitude, he resolved to share the secret only with those who truly deserved it.

Over the years, the deer led to the pond only those animals who helped others in spite of their own needs and acted ethically: a tiger who decided to stop eating meat, elephants who cared for orphaned calves, and a squirrel who shared its food with other creatures—all were granted a sip of the pond's water.

Word of this secret eventually reached Nalaka, who set out to find the deer. When he finally located him, Nalaka asked, "Why did you share the secret?" The deer replied, "It is not my right to keep such a gift to myself. Yet I make sure that only those who truly understand ethics and morality are allowed to drink."

Impressed by the deer's wisdom, Nalaka smiled and went on his way, assured that the pond's secret was in good hands.

MEANING & LESSON

This narrative underscores the importance of using privileges and resources responsibly and ethically. True morality reveals itself when one can wield power without exploiting it for selfish ends. It calls on us to place the welfare of all above personal gain.

SELF-REFLECTION

What would you do if you gained access to such a valuable resource?

_____
_____
_____

PRAJNA
THE PATH TO WISDOM

Wisdom, known in Buddhism as "Prajna," is far more than simply acquiring knowledge or possessing the ability to solve complex puzzles. It is a deeper understanding of the true nature of reality—an intuitive awareness that transcends mere thinking. Prajna illuminates the way through the dense forest of ignorance, guiding us toward enlightenment.

In the Buddhist tradition, Prajna is one of the three pillars supporting the path of the Bodhisattva—the being of enlightenment—alongside Ethics (Sila) and Meditation (Samadhi). Without Prajna, we might act and meditate without ever touching the deeper truths of our existence.

But how do we attain Prajna? How does this profound comprehension unfold in our lives? Stories help us grasp the essence of wisdom. Like mirrors, they reflect back to us both ourselves and the truths of life. They serve not only as educational tools but also as sources of inspiration, encouraging us to embark on the path of self-discovery and inner growth.

Let us now immerse ourselves in the world of Buddhist stories that reveal the heart of Prajna and inspire us to discover and nurture our own inner wisdom.

THE SEARCH FOR LOST WISDOM

In a remote village at the foot of the Himalayan mountains lived an elderly monk named Ananda. Renowned for his remarkable wisdom, he attracted visitors from near and far, all seeking his advice and benefiting from his teachings.

One day, a young man named Kavi arrived at the temple, brimming with enthusiasm. "Master Ananda," he declared, "I have heard of your great wisdom and have come to acquire it."

Ananda smiled gently and asked, "Why do you seek wisdom, young man?"

Eagerly, Kavi replied, "So I can lead a fulfilling life, help others, and be known as a wise man."

Ananda nodded. "Come back to me tomorrow morning, and I will share a secret with you."

Excited, Kavi returned at dawn. Ananda led him to a clear mountain lake and asked him to pick up a stone and toss it into the water. Kavi did as he was told, watching the concentric ripples spread across the surface.

"What do you see?" asked Ananda.

"I see ripples radiating outward from where the stone went in," Kavi answered.

"Wisdom," Ananda began, "is like this lake. Each action, each word, and each thought you have is like tossing a stone into these waters. Sometimes the waves are positive, sometimes negative. True wisdom enables you to understand the ripples of your actions and live in harmony with the lake."

Kavi felt puzzled. "But Master, how can I attain such wisdom?"

Ananda led him back to the temple and laid out an old, dusty book. "Read this book and find the lost wisdom," he said.

Months passed as Kavi diligently turned page after page, but he found no answers. Finally, discouraged, he returned to Ananda. "Master, I've read the entire book," he said, "but I haven't discovered any wisdom."

Ananda smiled again. "The book itself does not contain the wisdom you seek. Wisdom does not lie in words on a page. It is the result of reflection, experience, and understanding your own inner self. This book was merely a tool to encourage your introspection."

Suddenly, Kavi understood. He had expected wisdom to be something he could find like a treasure, but in truth it was a process of inner growth and self-discovery.

Bowing deeply before Ananda, he said, "Thank you, Master, for this lesson. I will spend my life seeking true wisdom through my own experiences and reflections."

Ananda nodded in satisfaction. "Go and live a life of awareness, Kavi. Wisdom will follow you."

And so Kavi left the temple—not with the treasure of wisdom he had hoped to find, but with the far more precious understanding of how to discover it within himself.

MEANING & LESSON

"The Search for Lost Wisdom" illustrates that true insight and wisdom are seldom found in the outer world; instead, they reside deep within ourselves. It reminds us to look inward and listen to our inner voice rather than constantly seeking guidance from external sources.

SELF-REFLECTION

"In which moments of your life have you searched for answers externally, only to realize later that the wisdom was already within you?"

_____

_____

_____

THE ECHO OF THE SILENT MOUNTAINS

In a small village at the foot of a towering mountain lived a young monk named Lin. The mountain had long been revered as a place of wisdom, and old legends spoke of a cave deep within it that held the answers to every question in life. Many people had ventured into the mountain's depths in search of this cave, but none ever returned.

Lin felt a powerful fascination with these stories. His heart burned with the desire to discover the source of true knowledge and profound wisdom. One morning, he decided to embark on the journey to the mountain's heart and find the legendary cave.

He packed a small bundle of food and water and set off. Days turned into weeks, weeks into months. Lin faced countless challenges—slippery trails, treacherous cliffs, and encroaching darkness. Yet his determination never wavered.

Finally, after a long and arduous quest, Lin found the cave's entrance. Venturing inside, he was not greeted by a hoard of books or sacred scrolls. The cave was empty, except for a pool of clear, still water in the center, reflecting light like a mirror.

Disappointed and exhausted, Lin approached the water, hoping for some sign or clue to hidden wisdom. Leaning over, he gazed at his reflection. Instead of seeing his tired face, he witnessed different versions of himself—as a child, as a teenager, and as an old man.

Memories flowed as he stared into the water. He saw his childhood, with its joys and sorrows and lessons learned. He saw himself as a teenager, brimming with dreams and aspirations. He saw himself as an old man, peaceful and content. Each stage of his life held experiences, insights, and flashes of clarity.

Suddenly, he understood: the cave did not hide wisdom in the form of books or scrolls. The wisdom lay within him—in his experiences, his memories, and the lessons he had gleaned from life itself.

With tears of realization in his eyes, Lin left the cave and returned to the village. Rather than speaking of his adventures or the cave's mysteries, he shared the lessons he had learned and the insights gained through self-reflection.

People soon came to understand that true wisdom cannot be found in hidden places or ancient writings, but in the depths of their own experiences and reflections. Lin had discovered not only the cave's wisdom but also the wisdom within himself. And that was the greatest gift he could offer— to his village and to himself.

MEANING & LESSON

"The Echo of the Silent Mountains" teaches us that genuine wisdom and clarity are often found in quiet moments of stillness, far from the distractions and noise of daily life. It encourages us to seek out silence regularly, to connect with our innermost selves, and to gain profound insights in the process.

SELF-REFLECTION

"When was the last time you listened to the echo of your own thoughts and feelings, instead of letting the world's clamor dictate your path?"

_____

_____

_____

THE WISE BUTTERFLY

In a dense, vibrant forest lived a small caterpillar named Kiri. Like all other caterpillars, Kiri spent most of her time eating leaves and preparing for the day she would transform into a chrysalis. Yet she was different from the other caterpillars—she was plagued by countless questions: "Why am I here?" "What is the purpose of life?" "Is there more to existence than just eating and sleeping?"

One day, as Kiri rested on a leaf, she overheard stories about an ancient, wise butterfly who lived at the top of the tallest tree in the forest. It was said that this butterfly possessed the world's wisdom and could answer any question.

Resolved to find answers to her deepest inquiries, Kiri began her journey up the colossal tree. She crossed rushing streams, climbed steep branches, and narrowly escaped hungry birds. After many days, she finally reached the summit.

There, bathed in a halo of radiant light, sat the old butterfly. Out of breath and overwhelmed, Kiri asked her questions.

The butterfly listened patiently, then replied, "Kiri, the answers you seek cannot be found in words. Look within yourself—within your own journey and transformation. That is where true wisdom lies."

Confused, Kiri pleaded for an explanation. The butterfly continued, "Every stage of your life, from caterpillar to butterfly, teaches you something. As a caterpillar, you learn patience and perseverance. In the chrysalis, in darkness and stillness, you learn to reflect and grow. And when you finally unfold your wings as a butterfly, you learn the meaning of freedom and transformation. The answers are not out there but in the lessons that every phase of your life offers."

Deeply moved, Kiri thanked the wise butterfly and made her way back down. Eventually, she wrapped herself in a chrysalis, reflecting on all she had learned. When she emerged as a beautiful butterfly, she understood the true meaning of wisdom.

She flew from tree to tree, from flower to flower, sharing her insights with others. Although she now enjoyed the freedom of the sky, she never forgot the profound lessons she had discovered on her journey to wisdom.

MEANING & LESSON

"The Wise Butterfly" tells a story of metamorphosis and of finding the courage to embrace transformation, even when the path forward is uncertain. It teaches us that true wisdom often emerges by accepting change and being willing to venture into the unknown.

SELF-REFLECTION

"How often have you resisted change out of fear of the unknown, only to realize later that those very changes led to deeper growth and wisdom?"

_____
_____
_____

SELF RESPECT

THE OFTEN OVERLOOKED VALUE

Self respect is the inner compass that guides us, allowing us to recognize and honor our own dignity. It lays the foundation for how we treat both ourselves and others, ensuring we respect our own boundaries and express our true selves. In the ancient Buddhist and Hindu teachings, self respect is seen as a virtue that arises not from pride or egotism, but from a deep understanding and acceptance of our true nature.

A person who respects themselves lives in harmony with their surroundings and radiates inner peace. In the following stories, we will explore the different aspects and dimensions of self respect and how it can influence our lives and our decisions.

THE DANCING BUTTERFLY

In a peaceful village at the edge of a dense forest, an annual festival took place where all the villagers showcased their talents. While people sang, danced, and demonstrated their skills, a young butterfly named Mira watched the spectacle from a safe distance.

Mira was not like the other butterflies. Instead of brightly colored wings, hers were dull and plain. The other butterflies often mocked her for this, so she hesitated to reveal herself to the villagers.

One day, as Mira sat quietly in a corner of the forest, a radiant light appeared before her. From the light emerged an old monk who asked, "Why do you hide yourself, little one?"

Mira told him about her simple wings and her fear of being ridiculed. The monk smiled and asked her to dance for him. With her eyes closed and a heavy heart, Mira began to dance, her wings fluttering in time with the beat of her heart.

When she opened her eyes, she saw that the entire forest was bathed in a gentle glow. Her simple wings had reflected the monk's light, illuminating the forest. "Your true beauty," the monk said, "is not in your appearance, but in your very being. All you need is the courage to show it to the world."

Encouraged by the monk's words, Mira performed at the next village festival, dancing with all her passion. The villagers were so captivated by her performance that they gave her a standing ovation. They had come to realize that true beauty flows from within.

MEANING & LESSON

We each carry a unique beauty and worth within us. Self respect means recognizing this inner light and sharing it bravely with the world. It is not our outward appearance, but our inner qualities that make us valuable.

SELF REFLECTION

When was the last time you hid your true self out of fear of rejection or criticism?

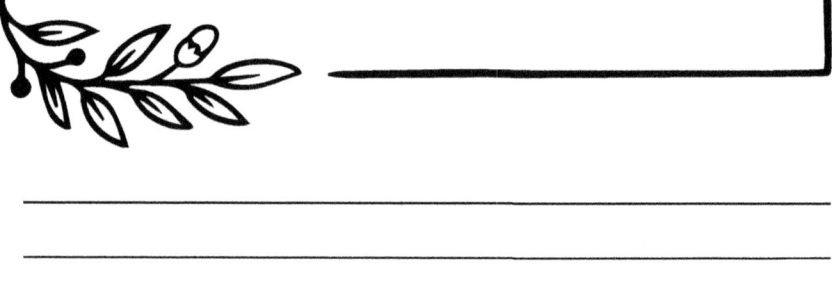

_____

_____

_____

THE SONG OF THE LOTUS

In a picturesque village at the edge of the Himalayas lay a lake famed for its magnificent lotus blossoms. What made this lake truly special was not just its beautiful flowers, but the fact that each lotus sang a soft, melodic song—audible only to those who truly listened within.

A young monk named Qoshi lived in a nearby monastery. Despite his daily meditation practice by the lakeside, he could not hear the lotus blossoms' song. His fellow monks, who claimed to hear the tune clearly, often teased him about it.

Disheartened and full of self-doubt, Qoshi one day retreated to a cave for deep meditation, searching for answers. Days passed. When he finally returned to the lake, he sat quietly at the shore, closed his eyes, and listened.

This time, he not only heard a single lotus's melody, but a harmonious concert of all the lotus blossoms together. He had come to understand that self respect is not about comparing oneself to others or seeking their approval. It is about finding one's own path and accepting that each person moves to their own rhythm and melody in life.

When Qoshi shared this realization with his fellow monks, many confessed that they had never truly heard the lotus song themselves—they had only pretended they could.

MEANING & LESSON

True self respect arises when we stop comparing ourselves to others and start appreciating our own uniqueness. It is essential to discover and embrace our own rhythm in life.

SELF REFLECTION

When was the last time you listened to your own inner song instead of comparing yourself to others' melodies?

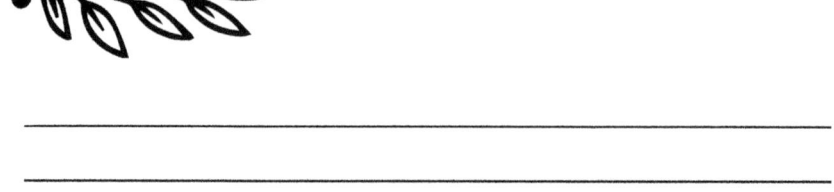

_____
_____
_____

SELF LOVE

EMBRACING YOUR TRUE SELF

Amid the hustle and bustle of everyday life—our constant striving for success and comparing ourselves to others—we often lose touch with our own being. Self love is not just a catchphrase or a passing trend but a vital practice deeply rooted in many spiritual traditions, including Buddhism and Hinduism. It involves recognizing, accepting, and nurturing oneself—physically and emotionally. To love oneself means treating yourself as you would a cherished friend, acknowledging your imperfections yet valuing yourself all the same. In this chapter, we delve into stories that highlight the importance of self love, teaching us how to better understand and appreciate ourselves, and reminding us why it's so crucial to love who we are. For only when we truly love ourselves can we genuinely love others and positively influence the world around us.

THE MIRROR OF THE SACRED TREE

In a remote forest in the heart of India stood a sacred banyan tree called Darpan Vriksha, or the Mirror Tree. Legend said that this tree could reflect a person's innermost self in its mirrored surface.

Travelers journeyed from far and wide, hoping to glimpse their true selves. Many returned disappointed, while others found enlightenment.

A young woman named Tara heard of this marvel and decided to see it for herself. Standing before the tree, she looked into the mirror and saw many versions of herself—as a child, a teenager, an old woman. Some images showed her laughing, others weeping, and still others in deep meditation.

Confused, she asked the tree, "Which of these images is my true self?"

In a gentle voice, the tree replied, "All of them, and none of them. Your true self is not only what you see, but also what you feel. Self love means accepting and embracing every aspect of your being."

Tara understood and left the forest filled with a deep sense of contentment and love for herself. She realized that self love did not mean seeking perfection, but rather accepting herself in all her dimensions.

MEANING & LESSON

Self love requires embracing every facet of who we are—both our light and our shadow. It's not about striving for perfection, but about seeing ourselves in our wholeness.

SELF REFLECTION

Which part of yourself do you find hardest to love, and why?

_____
_____
_____

THE SONG OF THE MOUNTAINS

In the foothills of the Himalayas lay a unique mountain peak, renowned for its distinctive trait—it echoed the words of every traveler who stood at its base.

A young monk named Omkar, wandering the mountains in search of enlightenment, came upon this summit one day. He had heard of the mountain's miraculous ability and decided to share his deepest sorrow with it. "I'm not good enough," Omkar called out. The mountain echoed back: "Not good enough."

Confused and disappointed, Omkar repeated, "I must be perfect." Again, the echo returned: "Must be perfect."

Tears filled Omkar's eyes as he feared he would never find the acceptance he sought, especially if even nature itself echoed his faults. But he remembered his master's teachings: "The world only reflects back what you put into it."

With new understanding, Omkar called out, "I love and accept myself as I am." The mountain's echo resounded, "Love and accept yourself."

A smile spread across Omkar's face. He realized the mountain was not emphasizing his shortcomings; it was simply mirroring his own thoughts and feelings.

MEANING & LESSON

The way we think and speak about ourselves powerfully influences our reality and sense of self. Self love begins with making a conscious choice to view and accept ourselves in a positive light, just as we are.

SELF REFLECTION

What message do you send yourself each day, and how does it shape your self-perception?

_____
_____
_____

THE RIDDLE OF THE PEACOCK

In a tranquil village in Rajasthan lived a splendid peacock named Mayura. Though Mayura had the most dazzling plumage in the entire village, he was never satisfied. He envied the eagle for its ability to soar, the cuckoo for its sweet song, and the peafowl for its strength.

Every day, he complained to the ancient banyan tree, "Why can't I sing like the cuckoo or fly like the eagle?" Each time, the wise old tree replied, "Mayura, everyone has their own gift."

Then one day, the goddess Saraswati appeared before Mayura and offered him a wish. Without hesitation, the peacock said, "I want to sing like the cuckoo."

His wish was granted. But with the cuckoo's voice, Mayura lost his magnificent plumage. Though he was pleased with his newfound talent, the village missed the dancing peacock with the gleaming feathers. Before long, Mayura realized that by chasing others' gifts, he had forfeited his own uniqueness.

Remorseful, he returned to the banyan tree for guidance. The tree spoke: "Acknowledge and cherish your own gifts, Mayura." Moved by Mayura's regret, Saraswati restored his plumage—yet allowed him to keep his cuckoo's voice as a reminder always to love and value himself.

MEANING & LESSON

It is natural to admire others and sometimes compare ourselves to them. Yet true self love emerges when we recognize and appreciate the uniqueness and beauty within ourselves. It is crucial to see and let our own light shine.

SELF REFLECTION

What unique gifts do you possess that you often overlook while admiring the qualities of others?

_____
_____
_____

MINDFULNESS

LIVING IN THE HERE AND NOW

In our fast-paced world—where technology and constant distractions are the norm—it's all too easy to feel disconnected from the present moment. We focus so often on the future or the past that we overlook the "now." Mindfulness teaches us to return to the present, notice the small wonders of everyday life, and cultivate a deeper sense of peace and connection with ourselves. This chapter offers stories that speak to the heart of mindfulness. They invite us to slow down, breathe deeply, and recall the simple yet profound joys of life. It's time to reconnect with the present moment and see the world with awakened eyes.

THE BUTTERFLY'S ECHO

In a remote mountain temple, deep in the forest, lived a Buddhist monk named Bodhi. Renowned for his deep meditation practice and mindfulness, Bodhi one day found himself visited by a butterfly that fluttered around him before finally resting on his shoulder.

Bodhi slowly opened his eyes, giving the butterfly his full attention. He observed the delicate patterns on its wings and the subtle movement of each fiber. He felt the light tickle of its tiny legs on his skin and heard the gentle flutter of its wings. Entirely without judgment or distraction, he immersed himself in that moment of pure awareness.

A passing traveler noticed the monk and the butterfly and stopped. "Why do you pay so much attention to this small insect?" he asked.

Bodhi smiled and replied, "In this butterfly, I see the entire universe. Mindfulness teaches me that in every moment, in every being, the whole world is contained."
Still puzzled, the traveler said, "But it's just a simple butterfly."

Bodhi nodded. "When you learn to greet every moment and every creature with mindfulness, you too will discover the universe in a single butterfly."

MEANING & LESSON

This story reminds us that mindfulness gives us the ability to perceive the depth and wonder of life in the simplest of things. It is an invitation to observe life with fully open eyes and find magic in every moment.

SELF REFLECTION

In which small moments or simple things could you discover the entire universe?

_____
_____
_____

THE RIDDLE OF THE STILL LAKE

In a secluded valley lay a crystal-clear lake, renowned as the most tranquil of all lakes. Despite being fed by roaring waterfalls and swift-running rivers, its waters remained perfectly smooth, without the slightest ripple.

One day, a young seeker arrived in the valley, drawn by the legends of the lake. He longed to uncover the secret of its stillness, hoping it would help calm his own restless mind.

For days, he meditated on the lakeshore, attempting to see into its depths, but he could not grasp its secret. Finally, in a moment of frustration, he cried out, "How can you stay so serene while my mind is in such turmoil? What is your secret?"

In response, he heard a gentle, whispering voice rise from the lake's depths: "I do not hold on to the rivers and waterfalls that flow into me. I simply allow them to pass through."

The seeker understood. He had been trying to control and hold onto his thoughts and feelings. But, just like the lake, he too needed to learn to let them flow through him.

MEANING & LESSON

This story shows that genuine inner peace does not come from controlling or suppressing our thoughts and feelings, but from recognizing them and allowing them to pass. Through mindfulness, we can learn to observe the constant stream of our thoughts without holding on.

SELF REFLECTION

Which thoughts or emotions are you clinging to that you might be better off letting go?

_____
_____
_____

THE CUCKOO'S SONG

At the foot of a mighty mountain lay a sacred forest where many hermits and monks meditated in solitude. In the heart of this forest lived a cuckoo with a distinctive voice. Each morning, it greeted the sunrise with its melodious call.

A young monk named Himani was especially fascinated by this bird. He noticed that the cuckoo sang only at daybreak and then fell silent for the rest of the day. Approaching the tree where the cuckoo perched, Himani asked, "Why do you sing only at the first light of dawn?"

To his surprise, the cuckoo answered, "Every moment is precious and unique. I sing to honor the moment of sunrise, then I spend the rest of the day in mindfulness and silence."

Himani was struck by the bird's wisdom. He realized that he often lost himself in thoughts of the past or the future, neglecting the present moment. Inspired by the cuckoo, he began to focus on the here and now, fully experiencing it in all its depth.

MEANING & LESSON

This story teaches that mindfulness invites us to be fully present in the here and now. By concentrating on the present moment, we can experience life in its entire richness and beauty.

SELF REFLECTION

How often do you let yourself be distracted by your thoughts and fail to appreciate the present moment?

_____
_____
_____

"Always act with mindfulness; the fruits of your actions are secondary."

— BUDDHA

"In the moment of mindfulness, the mind is neither grasped by desire nor by aversion."

— BHAGAVAD GITA

POSITIVE THINKING

THE POWER OF THOUGHT

In the endless ocean of the human mind, there lies a remarkable force we often overlook: the power of positive thinking. It is like a beam of light breaking through dark clouds, reminding us that hidden within every difficulty is an opportunity waiting to be revealed. Positive thinking does not mean ignoring reality or running away from challenges. Rather, it is a conscious decision to focus on the good and the possible. It is a tool that helps us cope with obstacles, strengthen our self-esteem, and reignite our joy in life. In this chapter, we dive into inspiring stories that illuminate the transformative power of positive thinking—showing us how it can guide us on our life's journey. May you find inspiration here and discover the radiant power that lies within each of us.

THE STONE OF LIGHT

In a small village lived a wise elder named Kushinagar. He carried with him a plain, round stone that everyone in the village called "The Stone of Light." Whenever someone felt despair, sadness, or hopelessness, they would visit Kushinagar and ask to see this stone.

A young traveler named Gayatri, who was passing through the village, became curious about this mysterious stone and asked Kushinagar if he could see it. Taking the stone from his pouch, Kushinagar placed it in Gayatri's hand. At first glance, the stone looked ordinary—dull and unremarkable. Disappointed, Gayatri asked, "Why do people call it the Stone of Light? It looks so plain."

Smiling, Kushinagar replied, "Sit down and hold the stone. Now close your eyes and think of a dark time in your life." Gayatri did as instructed. After a while, Kushinagar continued, "Now think of a bright, joyful time in your life." When Gayatri focused on a happy memory, he felt the stone grow warmer in his hand, radiating a gentle warmth. Opening his eyes, he looked at Kushinagar in amazement. "How is that possible?" he asked.

Kushinagar explained, "This stone reminds us that light and darkness are two sides of the same coin. When we focus on the light, on good times and positivity, we find warmth and comfort—even in our darkest hours."

MEANING & LESSON

Kushinagar's Stone of Light teaches us that even in the midst of darkness and challenges, there is always a spark of light and positivity to be found. The story encourages us to shift our perspective toward the good, discovering solace and hope when we need it most.

SELF REFLECTION

In what moments of your life have you focused on the positive to find comfort and hope?

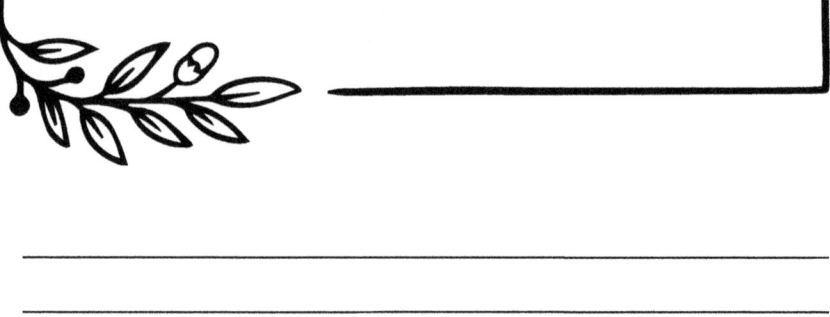

_____

_____

_____

THE SUNFLOWER OF BODHGAYA

In the sacred city of Bodhgaya—where the Buddha attained enlightenment—lived a monk named Dayan. One day, as he meditated outdoors, a gust of wind dropped a sunflower seed into his lap. On a whim, Dayan planted the seed beside his hut.

Each morning, he greeted the tiny plant and spoke loving words to it. Despite the scorching sun and occasional droughts, the plant continued to grow. Dayan noticed that no matter how fiercely the sun burned, the flower always turned toward the light, reaching for its rays.

Months went by, and pilgrims from all over the world arrived in Bodhgaya. One day, a pilgrim noticed the magnificent, towering sunflower and asked Dayan about the secret of its strength. Smiling, Dayan replied, "This flower teaches us a simple truth. Even when the world around it seems dark, it always seeks the light. Likewise, regardless of how dark our circumstances may be, we can direct ourselves toward the positivity—the light—in our lives."

MEANING & LESSON

Dayan's sunflower reminds us that, even in difficult times, we can choose to focus on the positive and the light. It underscores that our attitude and outlook are key to overcoming darkness and finding brightness in our lives.

SELF REFLECTION

Where do you turn when you feel surrounded by darkness?

_____
_____
_____

THE LION IN THE MOONLIT NIGHT

Deep within an unspoiled forest, many creatures lived together in harmony. However, unrest had filled the forest for several weeks because the lion—king of the jungle—had fallen into a deep melancholy. His gloomy thoughts cast a shadow over the entire forest, enveloping it in heaviness and darkness.

A small deer named Lina wanted to help. She began searching through ancient texts for wisdom and came across an old Buddhist parable. It taught that in every darkness a light is hidden, if only one learns to see it.

On a clear moonlit night, Lina led the lion to a clearing. The moonlight was reflected in a still pond, and Lina said, "Do you see how the moon reflects in this water even though it's thousands of miles away? In every darkness there's a light, just as in every problem a hidden opportunity can be found."

The lion gazed at the pond for a long time and, in the stillness of the night, felt a spark of hope awaken in his heart. He realized that he had been focusing too much on the darkness in his life and overlooking the ever-present light.

From that day on, the mood in the forest changed. The lion once again became a source of strength and inspiration, and the creatures lived together in renewed harmony.

MEANING & LESSON

This story reminds us that even in our darkest times, there is always a light to be found. It is vital to focus on that light and recognize the opportunities it brings, rather than be consumed by negativity.

SELF REFLECTION

Which "moonlit nights" in your life have helped you perceive the hidden light in your darkest moments?

_____
_____
_____

"What we think, we become. The mind is everything. What we think, we create."

— BUDDHA

"Watch your thoughts, for they become words. Watch your words, for they become actions. Watch your actions, for they become habits. Watch your habits, for they become your character. Watch your character, for it becomes your destiny."

— UNKNOWN

NON-SELF

ANATTA
EXPLORING THE TRUE NATURE OF OUR BEING

Within the profound teachings of Buddhism lies the concept of Anatta, often translated as "non-self." It is one of the three fundamental marks of existence, alongside Dukkha (suffering) and Anicca (impermanence). Anatta reminds us that all we label as "I," "mine," or "myself" lacks any enduring or independent essence. It challenges us to reflect on our deeply rooted notions of identity and self-worth—and to recognize how tightly we cling to them. By exploring "non-self," we learn to approach life from a place of letting go and selflessness, opening ourselves to a deeper connection with all that is, and freeing us to live more authentically. The following stories invite you to delve into this profound aspect of Buddhist teaching and consider how it may manifest in your own life.

THE LAKE'S REFLECTION

High in the mountains lay a clear and tranquil lake, known by the locals as "the Mirror of Truth." Because its waters were so calm and transparent, they perfectly reflected everything around them. Animals from far and wide came to catch a glimpse of their reflection in the lake.

One day, a magnificent peacock with shimmering feathers approached the lake. Having heard from other creatures how stunning he looked, he wanted to admire himself. But upon leaning over the water, he was disappointed to see a plain, gray figure gazing back. Confused, he asked the lake, "Why won't you show me my true beauty?"

An old, wise crane standing nearby answered, "The lake doesn't show you what you want to see—it shows you what you truly are. You are not just your brilliant feathers, but also everything that lies beneath them."

Humbled, the peacock realized that he was more than his outward appearance. He understood that what he considered "I" was fluid and could not be pinned down to any fixed identity.

MEANING & LESSON

This story reminds us that our identity and self-image are ever-changing, rather than set in stone. We must look beyond outward appearances and appreciate the deeper layers of who we are. By letting go of rigid ideas about ourselves, we can discover the true nature of our being.

SELF REFLECTION

When you peer into the lake, which expectations of yourself do you release in order to recognize the deeper truth of your being?

_____
_____
_____

THE PUZZLE OF THE BAMBOO FOREST

In a remote village stood a dense bamboo forest. Over the years, the villagers noticed something extraordinary about it: each bamboo stalk grew at exactly the same distance from the next, as though in perfect harmony.

One day, a curious traveler arrived and was captivated by this phenomenon. He asked the village elders about the forest's secret. An elderly monk led him to one of the bamboo stalks and said, "Touch this bamboo."

As soon as the traveler placed his hand on it, he felt the resonance flowing through the entire forest. The monk explained, "This bamboo teaches us about Anatta. Although each stalk appears separate, they are all connected through their roots. What you see as a 'single stalk' is actually just one manifestation of the entire forest."

The traveler understood: just like the bamboo, we humans are not truly isolated beings. What we call "me" is but a temporary appearance, constantly interacting with—and influenced by—the greater whole.

MEANING & LESSON

This story reminds us that our individual existence is deeply intertwined with the universe. The idea of a separate, solitary self is an illusion. Recognizing this can help us move through life with greater humility and a sense of belonging.

SELF REFLECTION

Which parts of your 'I' do you believe are truly isolated, and which arise from your connection to everything around you?

_____

_____

_____

THE RIDDLE OF THE GOLDEN MIRROR

In an ancient mountain temple called Dhvani Ashram stood a revered golden mirror, famed for its unique power: whoever looked into it would not see their own reflection, but that of another person.

Pilgrims from across the land journeyed there, hoping to solve the mystery of the golden mirror. Many believed that what they saw might represent a past life or a future incarnation.

One day, a wise yogi named Viran visited the temple. After gazing into the mirror, he smiled gently and sat down to meditate. Hours later, when he opened his eyes, the surrounding monks eagerly asked him to explain the mirror's riddle.

Viran said, "The mirror does not reveal our past or future lives. Instead, it shows the universal truth of Anatta. We habitually identify with an 'I,' yet in reality, no permanent self exists. What we view as 'I' is continuously changing, shaped by everything that surrounds us."

The monks understood. The mirror taught that what we perceive as our "self" is nothing more than an illusion—one constantly formed and reformed by experiences, thoughts, and emotions in endless flux.

MEANING & LESSON

This story illustrates that our notion of a fixed self is fleeting and ever-changing. Clinging to a rigid sense of "who we are" can lead to suffering. By recognizing the impermanence of our self-image, we cultivate a deeper understanding of Anatta and free ourselves from the constraints of self-identification.

SELF REFLECTION

How do you define your "I," and how has it changed over time?

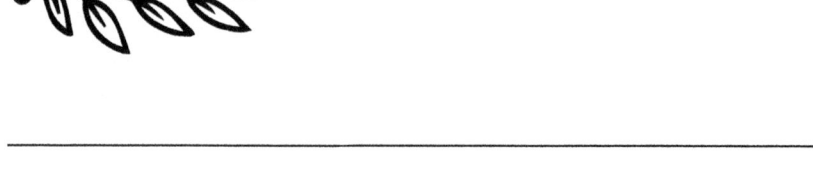

_____
_____
_____

"Form is emptiness, emptiness is form. Form is nothing other than emptiness, and emptiness is nothing other than form."

— BUDDHA

"Sabbe dhamma anatta" – *"All things (dhammas) are not-self."*

— UNKNOWN

EQUANIMITY

UPEKKHA

In the Buddhist tradition, equanimity—known in Pali as Upekkha—is regarded as one of the highest virtues. It is not about suppressing feelings or sensations, but rather about maintaining a deep inner balance and calm amid life's continual changes. In a world steeped in dualities—joy and sorrow, success and failure, praise and blame—Upekkha serves as an anchor, allowing us to remain stable and unshaken. It is the art of seeing things as they truly are, without being swept away or crushed by them. In the following stories, we'll explore the multifaceted nature of Upekkha and discover how it can help us navigate life's highs and lows with grace and wisdom.

THE VALLEY OF ECHOES

In a remote valley, known as the "Valley of Echoes," lived an old sage named Ravi. Legend held that any word called out in this valley would return as an echo of the same sound. People from near and far visited this place, releasing their wishes, fears, and secrets into the valley and listening to the echo of their own voices.

One day, a young woman named Saya arrived. She had faced much sorrow in her life and wanted to shout her pain into the valley, hoping the echo might bring her comfort. Raising her voice, she cried out, "Why has life brought me so much suffering?" The echo responded: "So much suffering…"

Sensing the pain in Saya's eyes, Ravi approached her and said, "Young lady, the echo returns only what you send it. It does not judge; it merely reflects."

Confused, Saya asked, "How can I find solace, then?"

Ravi replied, "Instead of hurling your sorrows and fears into the valley, call out words of gratitude, love, and hope. Then listen to what returns."

Saya took a deep breath and shouted, "Thank you for the lessons life has brought me!" The echo answered: "The lessons life has brought me."

A smile spread across Saya's face as she realized that equanimity lies not in changing the echo, but in choosing what she calls out.

MEANING & LESSON

This story reminds us that while we cannot always control what happens in life, we can control how we respond. Upekkha teaches us to approach life's ups and downs with calmness and wisdom, rather than allowing them to overwhelm us.

SELF REFLECTION

What are you calling into the valley of your life, and how do you receive its echo?

_____
_____
_____

THE QUEEN OF THE DESERT

Amid a vast desert of endless dunes lived a majestic lioness named Laya. She was known as the "Queen of the Desert," not only for her strength but also for her unshakable serenity in the face of the extreme desert environment.

One day, a curious vulture named Gara visited Laya and asked, "How can you remain so calm and content in a place this harsh? The searing sun, the relentless sandstorms—everything is so challenging!"

Laya smiled and replied, "Much like you fly without constantly worrying about the direction of the wind, I live in the here and now. I can't change the desert, but I can change my response to it. This is my home, and I've learned to meet its challenges with a peaceful heart."

Puzzled, Gara gazed into the distance. "But how do you find such tranquility when everything around you is in turmoil?"

Laya responded, "In the desert's stillness, I find my strength. By focusing on what I can control and accepting the rest as it is, I find peace."

Gara left the desert with a new perspective—and a sense of admiration for the lioness who maintained equanimity, even under the harshest conditions.

MEANING & LESSON

This story illustrates that equanimity does not depend on external circumstances but on our inner attitude. It is the art of living in peace and harmony, despite life's impermanence. By learning to accept the unchangeable and focusing on what we can influence, we can discover genuine inner peace.

SELF REFLECTION

In which "deserts" of your life could you practice greater equanimity by accepting things as they are?

_____
_____
_____

THE DANCING PEACOCK AND THE SILENT BAMBOO

In the dense jungle of an ancient Indian kingdom, a splendid peacock named Nandini would proudly display his shimmering feathers and dance with delight whenever the first monsoon rains arrived. Each time he danced, the animals gathered to marvel at his performance.

Close by grew a young bamboo tree, standing quietly without seeking attention. One day, Nandini couldn't resist teasing the bamboo: "Why do you stand there silently all day, never showing what you can do?"

Softly, the bamboo tree replied, "Dear Nandini, I take joy in being still and witnessing life's dance. It isn't always necessary to be in the spotlight. For me, it's enough to remain firmly rooted while reaching toward the sky."

Years passed, and the jungle was hit by a terrible drought. While many trees shed their leaves and the peacock no longer had the energy to dance, the bamboo remained green and strong. It offered shade, shelter, and even water from its hollow stems to the other creatures.

Humbled and grateful, Nandini realized the bamboo's strength and said, "Your equanimity and stillness are truly a form of dance—a dance of steadfast presence."

MEANING & LESSON

This story highlights the power of equanimity and how real strength often resides in silent steadfastness, rather than in showy demonstrations. It is a reminder that inner stability and calm can carry us through even the fiercest storms.

SELF REFLECTION

In which moments of your life could you shift from the peacock's flamboyant display to the bamboo's quiet equanimity?

_____

_____

_____

"Equanimity is the highest form of love. It is love without attachment."

– UNKNOWN

"Be equal in happiness and sorrow, in gain and loss, in victory and defeat. Then you will never sin."

– UNKNOWN

REBIRTH AND KARMA

In the deep philosophical teachings of Buddhism and Hinduism, rebirth and karma are two concepts inseparably connected. They offer answers to age-old questions about life, death, and what lies beyond. Rebirth —also known as reincarnation—is the idea that life continues after death in a new body, an endless cycle of birth, death, and rebirth. Karma, on the other hand, is the universal law of cause and effect: every action, whether good or bad, leaves an energetic imprint that manifests in this life or in future ones. Together, these concepts provide a profound understanding of life—its challenges and possibilities—reminding us that every action matters and that our lives today are shaped by past decisions, even as we create the foundation for future existences. In the following stories, we explore these deep ideas and reflect on their significance.

THE SONG OF THE WAVES

Along the bank of a sacred river—where pilgrims from across the land came to cleanse themselves in its waters—stood an ancient temple. Within it lived a wise old monk named Devan, frequently sought out for guidance and for the stories he told about the universe and its mysteries.

One day, Devan sat by the river's edge, watching the waves crash against the rocks. A young man named Trishna approached him and asked, "Master Devan, why do you spend so much time watching the waves?"

Smiling, Devan answered, "Each wave you see is like a life—born, living, then dying to make space for a new one. And yet the water from which the wave is formed remains the same."

Puzzled, Trishna asked, "But how does that relate to our existence?"

Devan explained, "Each life we lead is like one of these waves. We're born, we live, and then we die. But the essence, the soul, remains constant—just like the water. Our actions, our karma, determine the shape and direction of our next wave."

Thinking for a moment, Trishna asked, "How can we ensure that our next wave is peaceful and harmonious?"

Devan smiled. "By being mindful in every moment, by recognizing the consequences of our actions, and by striving for the well-being of all creatures. Like the water remaining calm even when the waves rage, we should stay steady and aware amid life's storms."

Trishna thanked Devan and departed, feeling a renewed sense of understanding and peace in his heart.

MEANING & LESSON

This story reminds us that, while our physical existence is impermanent, the essence of our soul endures. Our actions in this life shape the circumstances of our next life—and by practicing mindfulness and awareness, we can create positive waves in the vast ocean of being.

SELF REFLECTION

Which "waves" are you creating in your life, and how will they influence your future journey?

_____
_____
_____

THE DANCE OF THE BUTTERFLY

In a peaceful valley graced by a crystal-clear stream stood a remarkable tree that bloomed each year with thousands of shimmering butterfly cocoons. The villagers called it the "Tree of Souls," saying that each butterfly taking flight from its branches embodied the soul of a being newly reborn.

One morning, a young woman named Anya sat beneath the tree and watched a cocoon about to open. As the butterfly emerged, she noticed that one of its wings was injured, preventing it from flying.

Saddened, Anya gently lifted the butterfly and asked, "Why must you be born with a broken wing?"

Speaking in a soft voice, the butterfly replied, "In my previous life, I was a human driven by anger and jealousy. I hurt many and brought turmoil to their hearts. This wing is a reminder of the karma I carry into this life."

Astonished, Anya asked, "What can you do to fly again?"

The butterfly answered, "The remedy for my suffering does not lie in having a perfect wing, but in accepting my past and striving for kindness in this moment. By helping other creatures in the valley and spreading love and peace, I may fly more freely in my next life."

Anya nodded and placed the butterfly on a branch. She watched as it interacted with other beings in the valley, bringing joy and comfort despite its limitations.

MEANING & LESSON

This story highlights that our current state stems from past karma, yet acceptance and positive actions can release us from the shackles of the past. We all carry the weight of our former deeds, but through understanding, compassion, and right action, we can reshape our karma, setting forth on a path of healing and transformation.

SELF REFLECTION

What hurts from your past do you carry in your heart, and how can you transform them into wisdom and kindness?

THE VESSEL OF THE PAST

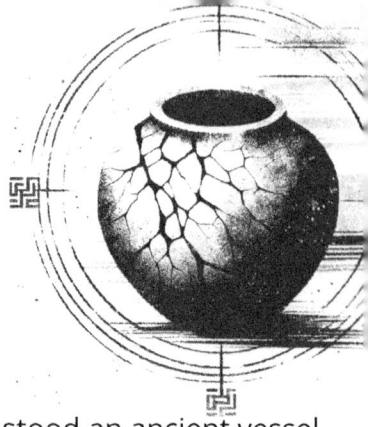

In a secluded mountaintop temple stood an ancient vessel known as the "Karma Jar." Rumor held that this jar had the ability to preserve the essence of past lives. Pilgrims traveled from far and wide for a glimpse into its depths, hoping to see echoes of their former actions.

One day, a solitary monk arrived at the temple. Approaching the jar with reverence, he bowed his head and peered inside. To his surprise, he saw none of the images from his past—only a clear, still liquid that shimmered like water.

Perplexed, he turned to the eldest temple guardian and asked, "Where are the memories of my deeds? Why does the jar show me only water?"

Smiling, the guardian explained, "The water in the jar reflects only this present moment. Its clarity reveals that you have let go of attachments and memories from past lives. You dwell now in the present, free from the chains of what has been."

Grateful for the revelation, the monk bowed. He understood that true insight and liberation do not come from sifting through the past, but from fully living in the present.

MEANING & LESSON

This story illustrates a core Buddhist idea: genuine liberation and understanding arise when we live in the here and now, unburdened by the weight of our past. Letting go of past attachments and focusing on the present is essential for experiencing true freedom and inner peace.

SELF REFLECTION

How deeply are you rooted in past memories and attachments, and how might you shift your focus to the present moment?

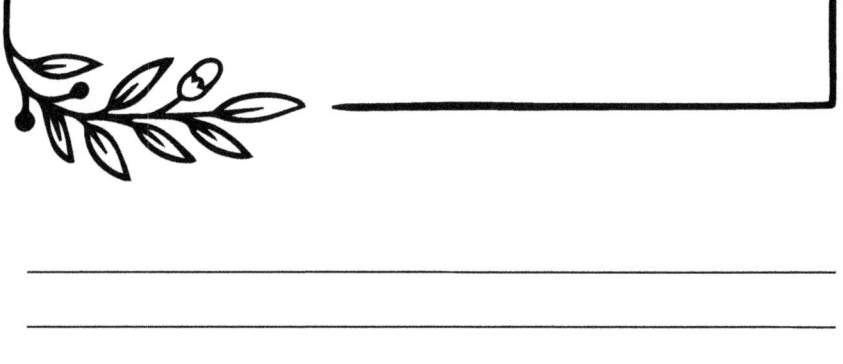

_____
_____
_____

SUFFERING AND ITS OVERCOMING

DUKKHA

At the heart of Buddhist teaching lies the concept of Dukkha, often translated as "suffering." Yet Dukkha encompasses far more than physical or mental pain. It refers to the inherent dissatisfaction arising from life's impermanent nature—the pain of craving and the endless search for something permanent in a world that is ever in flux.

Equally central to the Buddha's teaching is the path to overcoming this suffering. By recognizing the causes of Dukkha and following the Noble Eightfold Path, we can discover a route to liberation. This path does not require asceticism or fleeing from the world, but rather a deep understanding and transformation of our own mind and perceptions.

The following stories explore various dimensions of Dukkha and the possible ways to transcend it, offering glimpses into timeless insights and the chance for readers to apply these ancient truths to their own lives.

THE FLEETING PARADISE

Hidden in a secluded valley, surrounded by towering mountains, lay a paradise-like garden. So breathtaking was its beauty that those fortunate enough to find it often lingered at its edge, too awestruck to step further in. At its center, a small pond shimmered in the sunlight, filled with crystal-clear water dotted with elegant lotus blossoms.

One day, a wanderer—having searched and roamed for ages—finally discovered this garden. Overwhelmed by its perfection, he decided to remain there forever, convinced he had found an eternal haven. Days turned into weeks, and weeks into months. But as time passed, he noticed the flowers beginning to wilt, leaves falling, and the once-pristine pond filling with drifting leaves. Discontent crept in. The garden he believed to be everlasting perfection no longer seemed flawless.

Desperate, he sought out an old monk living at the valley's edge and lamented the loss of the garden's beauty and the inevitability of change.

Smiling gently, the monk said, "You loved the garden for what it was not: eternal and unchanging. True paradise does not lie in the forms you see, but in accepting the impermanence of all things. Find peace in constant change, and discover the beauty of each passing moment."

The wanderer grasped the monk's words and found solace in the garden's ever-shifting landscape. He realized that genuine happiness lies not in clinging, but in letting go and flowing with life's impermanence.

MEANING & LESSON

This story reminds us that nothing endures forever and that we should cherish the beauty of the present while finding peace in the inevitability of change.

SELF REFLECTION

Which moment in your life revealed the transience of all things, and how did you respond?

_____
_____
_____

THE DANCE OF SHADOWS

In a distant village, encircled by lofty mountains, an extraordinary event took place once a year. On a specific day, as the sun reached its zenith, shadows were cast in such a way that they appeared to move like dancing images. The villagers gathered annually to witness this phenomenon and shared stories about the shapes they saw in the shadows.

A wise hermit, living on the outskirts of the village, had heard of this spectacle and decided to witness it in person. On the appointed day, he sat with the villagers and observed the shifting shadows.

While everyone chattered excitedly and laughed, the hermit noticed tears in the eyes of a young woman. Gently, he asked, "Why do you weep on such a joyous occasion?"

She answered, "Each year, I see in the shadows the image of someone I loved who is no longer with me. The sight of that shadow reminds me of my sorrow."

The hermit nodded. "But don't you see? Shadows are fleeting. They come and go with the sun's movement. The same is true of our suffering. It is temporary and will eventually give way to the light."

Looking again at the dancing shadows, the young woman still felt her pain, but also recognized its impermanence. She realized that sorrow and joy coexist like light and shadow.

MEANING & LESSON

This story reminds us that suffering, like everything else, is impermanent. It encourages us to accept the duality of light and shadow, joy and pain, recognizing life's ever-changing flow.

SELF REFLECTION

How do you deal with the "shadows" in your own life?

_____
_____
_____

THE LABYRINTH OF EMOTIONS

Far from busy cities and towns, a mysterious temple stood in a remote region. Known by the locals simply as "The Labyrinth," legend held that those who entered would be confronted by their deepest fears, desires, and sorrows.

A monk, intrigued by this place, decided to enter the Labyrinth to gain a true understanding of Dukkha. With every twist and turn, his memories and emotions grew more vivid. He saw the unfulfilled wishes, missed opportunities, profound fears, and deepest anguish of his life.

Step by step, the burden felt heavier, and the monk could sense the weight of his emotions bearing down on him. Yet, instead of despairing, he took a deep breath and focused on the present moment. He realized that the memories and emotions he encountered were merely transient events—arising and passing.

With that realization, he finally found the Labyrinth's exit. Stepping into the daylight, he felt lighter, freed from the weight of suffering.

MEANING & LESSON

This story illustrates how facing our fears and suffering can help us overcome them. By recognizing their impermanence and remaining mindful in the here and now, we can liberate ourselves from the grip of Dukkha.

SELF REFLECTION

Which memory or feeling traps you in your own personal labyrinth?

_____
_____
_____

"There is suffering, but there is an end to suffering."

"I teach a path that leads to the end of suffering."

– BUDDHA

"The wise one, who does not rejoice in pleasure nor grieve in pain, who stands firm in the self—such a one has unwavering determination."

– BHAGAVAD GITA

IMPERMANENCE

ANICCA

In the ancient teachings of Buddhism and Hinduism, the recognition of impermanence holds a central place. Anicca, as it is known in Pali, refers to the constant flux and transformation of all phenomena. It reminds us that nothing in this world is permanent—whether it be joy or sorrow, gain or loss, life or death. While this understanding may initially seem unsettling, it also holds a profound liberation. By acknowledging and embracing the ceaseless flow of life, we can free ourselves from clinging desires and find deep inner peace and equanimity.

The following stories illuminate the many dimensions of impermanence, offering readers insights and perspectives on the continual coming and going of life's experiences.

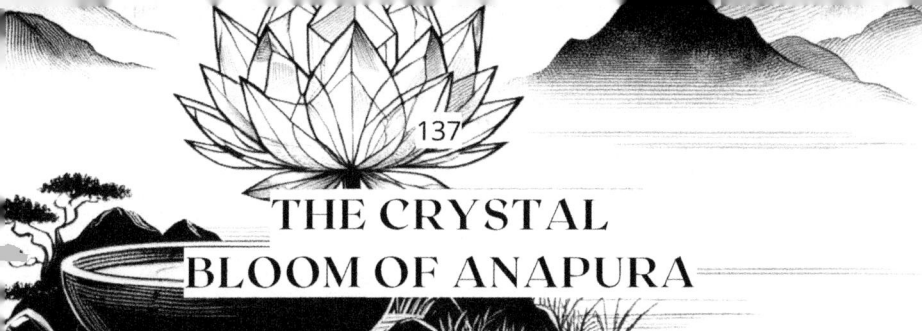

THE CRYSTAL BLOOM OF ANAPURA

In a secluded temple nestled in the mountains of Anapura grew a rare flower that bloomed only once every hundred years. Its petals glistened like crystal, and legend held that a single drop of its morning dew could grant a long and healthy life.

Monks and pilgrims from around the world traveled to this temple, hoping to witness the flower in bloom. As the anticipated year approached, crowds gathered at the temple. Among them was a young monk named Vajra, who was especially eager to behold the rare sight. He meditated near the flower for days, praying for the moment it would reveal its beauty.

On the day of the bloom, Vajra discovered to his dismay that the flower had already withered before he could see it in its full glory. Overcome with disappointment, he wept, feeling as though he had lost a once-in-a-lifetime opportunity.

An elder monk, Master Maitri, noticed Vajra's sorrow and sat beside him. "You are grieving for the flower, aren't you?" he asked gently.

Vajra nodded. "I've waited my whole life to see it, and now I've missed my chance."

Maitri smiled. "Life is full of such fleeting moments. The lesson is not in the flower's bloom but in its absence. Everything is transient, even our lives. Learn to appreciate the moment itself, rather than what it gives or takes from you."

Vajra pondered Maitri's words and found wisdom within them. The flower's impermanence had taught him a lesson that would endure: to embrace life's fleeting nature and find peace in the flow of change.

MEANING & LESSON

Everything in the world is impermanent. It is not the things we see or experience that matter most, but how we interpret and learn from them. True beauty often lies not in permanence but in the fleeting nature of life.

SELF REFLECTION

Which moment in your life did you cherish deeply, only to later realize its true meaning lay in its transience?

THE FADING COLORS OF MANDARA

High above the earth existed a mystical place called Mandara, a floating garden that held all the colors of the universe. Celestial beings flocked to Mandara to marvel at its vibrant hues and bask in its serene ambiance.

One day, the visitors noticed the colors of Mandara beginning to fade. The deep blues were the first to disappear, followed by the radiant reds and yellows. Concern grew as many attempted to restore the colors with their celestial magic, but none succeeded.

At the center of Mandara stood an old, unassuming well. Previously overlooked for its plain, colorless appearance, the well now began to emit a soft glow as the garden's colors waned.

A wise being named Luminara approached the well and peered into its clear waters. There, she saw not only the reflections of Mandara's colors but also the constant flow of transformation. She realized that the colors were not truly lost—they were merely changing, reshaping, and re-emerging in new forms.

Luminara shared her insight with the others: "Mandara teaches us an important lesson. Everything changes constantly, and clinging to a single form or color is an illusion. Let us embrace the beauty of transformation."

The celestial beings understood Luminara's wisdom and began to see Mandara not as a place of loss, but as a testament to the beauty of impermanence and transformation.

MEANING & LESSON

The world and everything in it are in a state of constant change. Instead of fearing or resisting transformation, we should embrace it as a natural and essential part of life. Impermanence is not the end, but the beginning of renewal and growth.

SELF REFLECTION

What in your life has changed, that you initially saw as a loss but later recognized as a necessary transformation?

_____
_____
_____

THE HOURGLASS VILLAGE

Beyond the seven mountains, in the heart of an endless desert, lay a unique village where all the houses were shaped like hourglasses. Inside each home were two chambers: an upper chamber filled with golden sand and a lower chamber that gradually filled as sand trickled down.

In this village, the sand did not flow with time but moved only through the intensity of lived experiences.

A young villager named Navin became obsessed with filling the lower chamber of his hourglass as quickly as possible. He rushed from one adventure to another, chasing every possible experience without pause. Yet, despite his efforts, the sand in his hourglass barely seemed to move.

One day, Navin met an elderly woman whose hourglass was nearly full, even though she spent most of her days quietly sitting in front of her house. Curious, he asked, "How did you fill your hourglass so quickly without constantly seeking new experiences?"

The old woman smiled and replied, "It's not the number of experiences that moves the sand, but the depth of each one. Instead of rushing from one moment to the next, I have learned to live each one fully and appreciate its richness."

Navin realized the wisdom of her words. In the days that followed, he slowed down, savoring the simple joys of life, admiring the beauty of the desert, and appreciating the flow of sand in his hourglass—no matter how slow it seemed.

MEANING & LESSON

It is not the quantity but the quality of our experiences that makes life meaningful. By fully immersing ourselves in the present moment, we can embrace the constant change and impermanence of life with grace and understanding.

SELF REFLECTION

Where in your life could you pause and truly feel the depth of a moment, instead of constantly seeking the next experience?

_____

_____

_____

"All compounded things are impermanent."

"Do not dwell in the past, do not dream of the future, concentrate the mind on the present moment."

– BUDDHA

"All that is transient is merely a parable."

– BHAGAVAD GITA

AFTERWORD AND REFLECTION

Dear Reader,

With this chapter, we conclude our journey through a vast ocean of wisdom, reflection, and self-discovery. This book was born out of a desire to make the essential concepts and ideas of Buddhism and Hinduism accessible through stories—stories that not only entertain but also inspire and encourage deep thought.

From the introduction to this very moment, we have explored themes such as Anatta, Upekkha, Dukkha, and Anicca together. Each story was an invitation to look into the mirror of your own soul, to view yourself, life, and the world around you from a new perspective. They provided an opportunity to delve into the deeply rooted teachings of these ancient traditions in a way that feels both contemporary and timeless.

The concept of impermanence, as explored in the story of the Sandglass Village, is just one example of how Eastern wisdom helps us embrace and appreciate life in its constant state of change. It reminds us that it is not the quantity but the quality of moments that makes life so valuable.

The engagement with themes such as "Self" and "Non-Self" or the exploration of Dukkha—suffering—may have challenged and enriched us simultaneously. Perhaps these reflections encouraged you to question your previous beliefs and assumptions, seeking a deeper, more authentic connection with yourself and the world around you.

As you close this book, we hope that it has not only entertained you but also sparked a glimmer of insight or inspiration. May each story, each Self-Reflection, and each theme continue to accompany you long after the last page is read.

Finally, we encourage you to continue this journey of self-discovery and inner growth. May your heart always remain open to the infinite possibilities of self-awareness, and may your mind forever have the courage to explore the depths of your own existence.

With gratitude and connection,
Savita Yara

Imprint

English First Edition, December 2024
Copyright © 2024 Savita Yara

All rights reserved.

Reproduction, even in part, is not permitted. This work, including its components, is protected by copyright. Any use without the publisher's and author's consent is prohibited. This includes, in particular, electronic or other reproduction, translation, distribution, and public accessibility.

The pseudonym Savita Yara is represented by: Matthias Kupka, c/o IP-Management #47599, Ludwig-Erhard-Str. 18, 20459 Hamburg, Germany

Manufacturer and Publisher: Independently Published

1st Edition

ISBN: 9798305151206

Printed in Great Britain
by Amazon

"Always above, seldom on the same level, never below"

— Edward Mannock

CONTENTS

Getting My Wings	1
Prisoner of War	9
My German Friend	16
Banquet at Courtrai	26
A Great Escape	37
Traipsing through Germany	42
Adventures in Luxembourg	46
A Hunted Animal	52
Wandering through Belgium	60
Confronting German Soldiers	66
My Counterfeit Passport	72
Through the Keyhole	84
Moving Picture Show	91
Village Under Attack	96
Approaching the Border	99
Getting into Holland	105
Streets of Rotterdam	111
Meeting the King	119
Back Home Again	122
Author's Note	125
Also by War History Journals	127

GETTING MY WINGS

I started flying in Chicago in 1912. I was 18 years old and always wanted to be a pilot. When I was younger, I followed the exploits of the Wright brothers with significant interest. I have to admit, I sometimes hoped they wouldn't have conquered the air until I had a chance at it myself.

I got my chance later on in life. My parents were opposed to me risking my life at what they said was the most hazardous pastime a young man could choose. Whenever I had a smash-up or some other accident, I was ordered to never go near the aviation field again. So I went to California.

I went with a friend, and we built our own plane. We flew all over the state. Back in early 1916, trouble was brewing in Mexico. I joined the American Flying Corps and was sent to San Diego. Where at that time, the army flying school was located. I spent eight months there, but I was anxious to get into active service. It didn't seem like America had much chance of getting involved in the war. I decided to resign and cross over to Canada. I joined the RFC (Royal

Flying Corps) in Victoria, B.C. I was sent to Toronto to receive instruction.

When I was a cadet, I made the first loop ever made by a cadet in Canada. After I performed this stunt, I thought I'd surely get kicked out of the service for it. To my surprise, they allowed me to teach the loop as part of a regular course of instructions for cadets in the Royal Flying Corps.

In less than nine months, eighteen of us officers left for England. If any of us were older than twenty-five, they'd concealed themselves well. The RFC didn't accept older men as pilots. We were made up of nine Englishman and nine Americans. Most of my fellow Americans were tired of waiting for our country to join the war, and we were able to join the British colors out of Canada.

In May 1917, we were off to earn our Wings. It was a qualification we had to earn before we were allowed to hunt Germans on the western front. Within a few weeks of arriving in France, we'd won our Wings. We wore our insignia with pride on our left breast. By August, the majority of us were full-fledged pilots and actively engaged the enemy in daily conflict.

While in France, we were sent to a place known as the Pilots Mess. Here we gathered with training squadrons from Canada and England to await assignments to particular squadrons we were to join. The Pilots Mess was set back a few miles in the back of the lines. Whenever a pilot was shot down or killed, the Pilots Mess was notified to send another to take his place.

The casualty rate in the RFC was atrocious. The demand for new pilots was unquenchable. Every new pilot itched to get into the fight as badly as I did. We became impatient. We realized every time they called up a new man; it meant that someone else had probably been killed, captured, or wounded. Early one morning an order came in for a scout pilot, and one of my friends was assigned. I remember how envious I was of him. At the time, it felt like it was the last chance any of us would get to the front.

Only three hours passed before I received a wire at the mess. I was ordered to follow my friend. I learned afterward that as soon as he arrived at the Squadron; he asked the commanding officer to wire me to join him. At the Pilots Mess, it was the custom of officers to wear shorts. They're about eight inches long, like what the Boy Scouts wore. They left a space of about eight inches of open country between the top and the end of the shorts.

The Australians wore them at the Dardanelles. I was wearing these shorts when the order came in for me, and I didn't have time to change into any other clothes. I couldn't wait to get to the front. If I'd been in my pajamas, I would have gone that way. I threw an overcoat on in the rain. I made record time to the aerodrome where I was ordered to report. I leaped from my automobile, and my overcoat blew open, displaying my shorts. Instead of the regulation flying breeches, I was supposed to be wearing. I made quite a commotion in camp.

"Must be a Yank." One officer said to another as I walked up, "nobody but a Yank would have the cheek to show up that way." They smiled and laughed good-naturedly as I came up to them. They welcomed me into their Squadron. They made me feel at home. My Squadron was one of the four stationed about 20 miles back of the Ypres line. We had 18 pilots in our Squadron. We only had one mission. We went out in the sky and picked fights. We were expected to pick fights and not wait until they came to us. When the bomb droppers would go over the lines in the daytime, the Scout Squadron would fly with them as convoys. The bomb droppers flew at 12,000 feet, and we were 1,000 feet above to protect them.

We protected them and fought off enemy planes. If at any time the bomb droppers were attacked, it was the duty of the Fighting Scout Squadron to dive and fight. The orders of the bomb droppers were to go on dropping bombs, and not to engage or fight unless they absolutely had to. There was rarely a time that the bomb droppers weren't attacked when they got over enemy territory. Our Squadron had plenty of work to do. In addition to airborne combat, our Squadron was under constant bombardment from the ground. We were trained well and knew how to avoid getting hit from the ground.

For my first flight with the Squadron, I was taken out over the lines to get a look at things. I needed to map out my location in case I was ever lost. I had to locate lakes, forests, and other landmarks to get the lay of the land. Other pilots insisted I knew the location of hospitals. If I was ever wounded and could pick my landing, I needed to land as near as possible to a hospital. These are all things a new pilot goes through during the first two or three days of joining the Squadron.

Our regular flights consisted of two a day. Each flight lasted for two hours. After our routine patrol, it was up to us if we wanted to go out on our own before heading back to the Squadron. I found out quickly that my Squadron was an elite group. Our pilots were always assigned special duty, such as shooting up enemy trenches, sometimes at only 60 feet off the ground.

This is how I received my baptism of fire. It was the third

time I went out over the lines. I was excited for a fight. The thought of being attacked by hostile plane above and also swept by machine gunfire from below captivated me. Some of our planes came back so riddled with bullets that I wondered how they ever held together. Before we flew, we were careful to make sure our motors were in perfect condition. Because they told us the *war-bread* was awful in Germany.

It was one morning after I joined the Squadron, and three of us started over the line on our own accord. We watched four enemy aircraft coming toward us. These two-seater aircraft were used by the Germans for artillery and bomb dropping. We knew they were bent on mischief. Each plane had a machine gun in front, worked by the pilot. The observer also had a gun that could spray all around. When we first noticed them, our planes were about six miles behind the German lines. We were laying up high in the sky, keeping the sun behind us so the enemy couldn't see us. We picked out three enemy German planes and dove on them. I flew close to the man I picked for myself. His observer in the rear kept pumping out bullets at me. Not one of my shots hit, and I went under him, but I turned and gave him another burst of bullets. He went down in a spinning nosedive. One of his wings went one way and then another. I watched as he crashed to the ground. I knew I had scored my first hit on an enemy plane.

One of my comrades also scored a hit, but the other two German planes got away. We chased them until things got too hot for us, but we had to call it a day. This first experience whet my appetite for more to come. I didn't have long to wait.

A few years ago, a spinning nosedive was considered one

of the most dangerous things a pilot could attempt. Many men were killed getting into the spin and not knowing how to come out of it. Several pilots thought that once you got into a spinning nosedive, there was no way out. It's now used in actual flying. The planes we used in France are controlled in two ways, by hands, and by feet. The feet work the rudder bar or the yoke. This controls the rudder that steers the aircraft. The lateral controls and fore and aft, causing the plane to rise and lower, are controlled by the joystick.

When you're flying, a pilot should hold on to the stick, so it'll gradually come back toward the pilot. In that position, the aircraft will climb. This means if a pilot is shot and loses control of his joystick, his plane will ascend until the angle formed becomes too great for the motor to pull the plane. In a fraction of a second, it stops. The motor being the heaviest causes the nose of the aircraft to fall forward, pitching down at a horrific rate of speed, spinning at the same time. If the motor continues to run, it increases speed and the wings could double up, causing the aircraft to break apart.

These spins are typically done with the motor on. You'd descend like a ball being dropped from the sky. This increases the velocity with the power of the motor and the spinning nose, frequently used in stunt flying. Now, it's been put to practical use by pilots getting away from hostile aircraft. When a plane is spinning, it's almost impossible to hit him. It makes the attacker think his enemy is going into a death spin. If the pilot does this over his own lines, he can right his machine and come out of it. But if this happened in German territory, they'd follow him down, and when he came out of the spin, they'd be above him with the advantage and shoot him down quickly.

It was a good way to get into a cloud and used very often.

The amount of courage and skill required by the pilot makes it challenging to come out alive. It's difficult to tell whether it's forced or intentional until the pilot rights his aircraft and comes out of it or crashes.

Another dive similar to this one is just known as a plane dive. It's when a pilot flies at a height of several thousand feet, gets shot and loses control of his aircraft. The nose of the plane heads downward with the motor full on at a tremendous speed. He goes swift and straight at a speed too fast for the aircraft. The planes weren't constructed to withstand enormous pressure forced against their wings, and they crumble up. If you try to straighten the plane, the elevators become affected. This happens when trying to bring your aircraft out of a dive. This strain is too much for the wings, and the results are disastrous. If a fuel tank is punctured by a tracer bullet from another aircraft, the plane catches on fire and goes into a straight dive at hundreds of miles an hour in a ball of flame.

The spinning nose dive was used by the Germans to a greater advantage than our pilots. The reason is that if a fight gets too hot for the Germans. He'll put his aircraft into a spin. We'd usually be fighting over German territory. He spins down out of our range and straightens out before he reaches the ground. It's foolish to follow him down inside German lines because you'll probably get shot down before you can get sufficient altitude across the line again.

Often a pilot will be chasing another aircraft when suddenly he starts to spin. Sometimes they're fifteen to eighteen thousand feet in the air, and the hostile aircraft spins down for thousands of feet. The pilot thinks he's hit the other plane and goes home happy that he brought down another German. He reports what happened to the Squadron, telling them how he shot down the enemy aircraft. But when the rest of the Squadron comes in or an artillery observation balloon reports. It's often the case that the German pilot only a few hundred feet from the ground came out of the death spin and flew enthusiastically for his own lines.

PRISONER OF WAR

It was the morning of August 17, 1917. Our Squadron crossed the line on an early morning patrol. The first thing I saw was two German balloons. I never saw a balloon from this distance before. I decided after my patrol, I'd go off on my own and see what these German balloons looked like up close.

These observation balloons were used on both sides. Crews sat in balloons and directed artillery fire through their vantage point. They followed artillery bombing and reported back on enemy movements. One of our primary missions was to shoot down those balloons.

There are two ways of attacking a balloon. One of them is to fly close to the ground, so the anti-aircraft guns can't fire at you. You continue flying along until you get to the level of the balloon. If you haven't drawn the balloon down by now. You open fire, as you score hits the bullets set the balloon on fire. The second way is to get close to the balloon. Then put your aircraft into a spin. Once you get above them, spin over the balloon and open fire. Afterward, quickly fly back across the line at 100 feet. This was one of the hardest jobs I had in the war. This is much more dangerous than attacking enemy planes.

I made my mind up to attack these balloons or make them descend. I hoped they were still there waiting for me so I could have a whack at them. After my two-hour duty was up, I dropped out of the formation and turned back. I was at fifteen thousand feet, much higher than the balloons. I shut my motor off and dropped through the clouds, hoping to find balloons at about five or six miles behind German lines.

I pulled out of the cloud bank and saw a two-seater German aircraft who looked like he was doing artillery observation and directing German guns one thousand feet below me. I was four miles behind the German lines. The artillery spotted me. They put out ground signals to attract the enemy pilot's attention. I watched as the observer grabbed his gun, and the pilot stuck the nose of his aircraft straight down. They weren't fast enough to escape me. I dove toward them at two hundred miles an hour, shooting all the way down at them. Their only chance was if the force of my dive broke my wings. I knew this was dangerous, but as soon as I came out of my dive, the Germans would have their chance to get me. I had to get to them first and take my chances. Luckily, some of my first bullets found their mark. I came out of my dive at four thousand feet.

The German plane never came out. Then came the toughest situation in the air I'd ever experienced. The depth of my dive brought me within reach of their machine guns on the ground. They fired a barrage of shrapnel at me from their anti-aircraft guns. I was able to *ride the barrage* as we call it in the Royal Flying Corps. Next, they fired Flaming Onions at me. Flaming Onions are rockets fired from a rocket gun used to hit low-flying aircraft. Their effective range is only forty-five hundred feet.

Most of the time, they're shot up one after the other in strings of eight. If they hit the aircraft, it's bound to catch fire, and then the jig is up. I was also attacked by—*Archie*—anti-aircraft fire. I escaped the Flaming Onions, but Archie hit me five times. Every time I was plugged by a bullet, it made a loud bang because of the tension on the material covering the wings. I wasn't seriously hit until I was over a mile away from our lines, and they hit my motor. I still had enough altitude to drift over to our side of the lines, but my motor was entirely out of commission.

They fired at me the whole time I descended. I thought I'd crash before crossing the line, but a slight wind in my favor carried me a couple miles behind our lines. Those damn balloons I'd gone out of my way to find were now pinpointing my exact location to the artillery. There are two men stationed in each balloon. They generally ascend to at least several thousand feet about five miles behind their own lines and are equipped with a signaling apparatus. They watch their artillery bursts, recheck position, get range, and then direct the next shot. If the conditions are favorable, they're able to direct artillery shelling and almost always destroy their intended target. This type of balloon got my position, called in for an artillery bombardment, and shelled my plane. If I'd destroyed the two balloons instead of the airplane. I probably wouldn't have lost my aircraft and would've made it home.

I landed on terrain that was covered with wide, gaping shell holes. Even though I had a forced landing, my aircraft was not severely damaged. I jumped out and walked around to see exactly where the damage was. It could easily be repaired. I could fly on from here, If I could find a space long enough between the two shell holes and get a head start before leaving the ground. I examined my plane and considered how to go about the few repairs. I didn't think of my own safety in this unprotected spot. A shell whizzed through the air. It knocked me to the ground and landed a few feet away. I pushed myself up and ran for cover. If I hadn't tripped and fallen into a shell hole, I'd have gotten farther away. I had no idea where the next shell would burst. I squatted down and took cover and let them blaze away.

The only injury I suffered was from the mud that splattered in my face over my clothes. That was my first introduction to this shell hole. I decided right then and there that the infantry could have all the trench and shell hole fighting they wanted. It was not for me. The infantry lived in them for many long nights, and I'd only sheltered in one for a few minutes.

The Germans had utterly demolished my aircraft and ceased fire. I waited for a short time. I was afraid they might send over a lucky shot and get me after all. But apparently, they decided they'd wasted enough shells on only one man.

I cautiously crawled out and shook the mud off. I looked over where my plane had once been, there wasn't even enough left for a souvenir. I headed back out on my way to infantry headquarters, where I was able to telephone in to report. Not long after, one of our automobiles came out and took me back to our aerodrome. Most of my Squadron thought I was killed or captured. They never expected to see me again except for my one friend, Owen Wrinn. He held out that I was going to be alright.

I learned later he told the commanding officer not to send for another pilot. He said, "that American will be back if he has to walk." The only thing that kept me from walking was the fact that our own automobile had been set out to bring me back. I learned many things and had lots to think about that day. I shouldn't have been so cocky in my own ability. One of the pilots in my Squadron told me I shouldn't take those types of chances; it was going to be a long war. I'd have plenty of opportunities to get killed without forcing it on myself. Later I learned the literal truth of his remark.

Later that night, my Flight (each Squadron is divided into three Flights of six men) was tasked to go out again. I got dressed and noticed I wasn't marked up for duty. I found the commanding officer, a major, and asked him why. He said I'd done enough for one day. But I knew if I didn't go, someone else from another Flight would take my place. I insisted on being able to go. The major reluctantly agreed. If I'd have known what was in store for me, I'd have stayed put.

We crossed the lines. And one of our planes dropped out because of motor trouble. Now we only had five aircraft for this patrol. At 7:50pm, we flew above fifteen-thousand feet and saw three other British aircraft a thousand feet below us pick a fight with eight German planes. Right then and there, it dawned on me that we were in for it. Over toward the ocean, there was a whole flock of German aircraft, which our scrappy comrades below us hadn't seen. We dove on those Germans.

The fighting at first was even. It was eight on eight. But the other aircraft in the distance flew over at a higher altitude than us and arrived on the scene. They dove on us. There were now twenty of them versus our eight. I looked over my shoulder and noticed that four of them singled me out. I went into a dive. They dove right after me, shooting as they came. The tracer bullets inched closer to me every second. My stomach dropped, and my forehead was slick with sweat.

Those tracer bullets were like balls of fire that allowed the shooter to follow a course and correct their aim. They wouldn't do any more harm to a pilot than an ordinary bullet. But if they hit the gas tank. It's over. When an aircraft catches fire in flight, there's no way of putting it out. It takes less than thirty seconds for the fabric to burn off the wings, and then the aircraft drops like an arrow, and leaves a trail of smoke like a comet.

A few days before I flew over the line, I watched a fight above me. A German aircraft caught fire and dove through our formation in flames on its way to the ground. The German dove at such a sharp angle that both his wings ripped off. We passed within a few feet of each other. I'll never forget the look of pure terror on his face. In seconds, I expected to suffer a similar fate. The tracer bullets came closer. I realized my chances of escape were zero. The very next shot hit me. The look on that Germans face flashed through my mind. I had only one chance. I needed to make an Immermann turn.

This maneuver was invented by one of the greatest German pilots ever, who was ultimately killed in action. I made this turn magnificently and brought one of their aircraft right in front of me. I had the drop on him. When I close my eyes, I can still see his startled eyes and white face. He must have known his last moment had come. His position prevented him from aiming at me while my guns pointed straight at him.

My first tracer bullet passed within inches of his head. The second looked like it hit his shoulder. The third struck him in the neck. I let him have the whole works, and he went down in a spinning nosedive. Through all this, three other German aircraft were shooting at me. I heard bullets striking my plane one after the other. I knew I couldn't beat off the remaining three Germans, but there was nothing for me to do but fight. My hands were full. I glanced at my instruments and my altitude. I was at eighty-five hundred feet. A burst of bullets went into the instrument board and blew it away to smithereens.

Another bullet tore through my upper lip. It came out of the roof of my mouth and lodged in my throat. I spun. I didn't feel any pain, and it all happened so fast. I yanked back on the joystick as hard as I could. I started to level out. There were trees everywhere. I kept leaning forward, and closing my eyes, I was so tired. The heat from the warm blood dribbled down my chin. The ground came up to meet me so fast, I closed my eyes and pulled back on my joystick with all the strength I could muster. My hands were slimy and slippery with blood.

I woke up in a German hospital at five o'clock the next morning. I was a prisoner of war.

MY GERMAN FRIEND

The makeshift hospital I found myself in was filthy. It shouldn't have been used as a hospital. It looked like it had only been used for a few days because of the big push taking place. They would probably abandon it as soon as the Germans found a better location. The house had five rooms and a stable, the biggest space in the house. I never looked into this particular wing of the hospital.

I was told that it was already overfilled with patients lying on beds of straw on the ground. I wasn't sure if they were officers or privates. I found myself in a room which had eight other beds, four of which were occupied by wounded German officers. I imagined in the other rooms they had the same amount of beds as mine.

I didn't see any Red Cross nurses, only orderlies. Probably because this was an emergency hospital and too close to the front for nurses. The orderlies weren't old men or young boys. They were strong young men in the prime of their life, who had probably been medical students. There were even a couple that could speak English. They refused to talk for some reason, most likely forbidden by the officer in charge.

The bullet wound in my mouth ached. My forehead swelled, and the back of my head was as big as my shoe. Every inch I moved was met a lightning bolt of intense pain. The doctor told me I didn't have any broken bones. I wondered how much worse I'd feel if I did. A couple German officers visited me that morning. They told me that my aircraft went down in a spinning nosedive from a height of eight thousand feet. They were shocked when they discovered I hadn't been ripped to shreds. They cut me out of my plane, which was riddled with bullets and shattered into pieces. The German doctor that removed the bullet from my throat asked me when I woke up if I was an American.

I couldn't deny it because I wore the metal identification disc on my wrist with the inscription Lieutenant Ryan, USA, Royal Flying Corps. I was in intense pain. The doctor spoke perfect English and insisted on talking to me. "You're no better than any common murderer," he said. "Any Americans who got into this war while their country stayed out of it are criminals and should be treated as such."

I couldn't answer him because of the wound in my mouth. I was already suffering too intense a pain, to be hurt by anything he could say. He asked me if I wanted an apple. I thought I could just as easily eat a brick.

"You won't have to worry anymore," he said, "The war is over for you." He stomped off when he didn't get any answers from me. They gave me a little broth later that afternoon. I collected my thoughts and wondered what happened to my comrades in the battle, which had such disastrous results for me. I realized my plight and became less worried about my physical condition. I'd only been in it for a short time. And now, I was going to be a prisoner for the duration of the war.

The next morning, more German officers came to visit me. They treated me well. They told me about the man I'd shot down, they said he was a good pilot and a Bavarian. They gave me his jacket as a souvenir and complimented me on my fighting skills. My soft leather helmet was split from front to back by a bullet from a machine gun. They examined it with curiosity and brought me my uniform. My Lieutenant's rank star on my right shoulder strap was cleanly shot off. They asked if they could keep it as a souvenir. I gave it to them.

They allowed me to keep my Wings. Even the Germans were aware that that is the proudest possession of a British Flying Officer. I believe I'm right when I say that the only chivalry in this war on the German side of the trenches was displayed by the officers of the German Flying Corps. They were the elite of their country's military. They pointed out that me and my comrades were fighting only for the love of it, where they fought in defense of their country. I debated asking them if by dropping bombs on London and killing all those innocent people was in defensive of their country. But I was in no condition to pick a fight.

Another German officer was brought into the hospital and put into the bunk next to me. I glanced over at him but didn't pay any particular interest to him at the time. He laid there silently for over four hours before I turned over and took a real good look at him. I was sure he couldn't speak English, so I didn't say anything to him. I turned my head again over in his direction and his eyes were on me.

"What the hell are you looking at?" he said and then smiled and winked.

I stumbled a few words out, but my wound made talking

difficult. I told him how I happened to be there. He'd already heard my story from some other German officers. He told me it was too bad I hadn't broken my neck. Apparently, he didn't have much sympathy for the Royal Flying Corps.

He asked me where I came from in America. When I told him, San Francisco, he asked, "How'd you like to have Sunday Brunch at the Cliff House?"

I told him my mouth was in no shape to eat anything right about now. I asked him what he knew about the Cliff House, and he said, "I was connected with that place for many years, I ought to know all about it." After that, we became pretty good friends. We spent hours talking about the days we spent in San Francisco. Sometimes we'd mention some Californian or other incidents that we knew about. He told me he was patriotic. When the war started, he chose to go back and defend his country.

He couldn't go directly from San Francisco because the water was too well guarded by the English, so he boarded a boat for South America. He found a forged passport in the guise of a Montevidean and took passage to New York. From there he flew to England. He passed through England easily with his fake passport but decided not to risk going into Holland. He didn't want to make anyone suspicious.

He went down through the Strait of Gibraltar into Italy, neutral at the time, up through Austria and then into Germany. When his ship pulled into port at Gibraltar after leaving England, two men were taken off the ship that he was sure were neutral. His passport and credentials were examined and passed without a problem. He spoke of his trip from America to England as pleasant. He had a great time because he connected with the English passengers on board. His fluent English got him into several arguments on the subject of the war. He was a hit one evening when the crowd assembled for a little music. He suggested they sing *God Save the King*. After that, his popularity skyrocketed. An English officer came up to him and said, "It's too bad we don't have men in our army like you."

He agreed it was too bad because he could have done more for Germany if he'd been in the English army. In spite of all of his apparent loyalty. My German friend didn't seem very enthusiastic about the war. He admitted that the political battles waged in California were much more to his liking than the battles he'd gone through over here. And then on second thought, he left as though it was a good joke. He wanted me to understand that he'd taken a keen interest in San Francisco politics. When my German friend first started this conversation, the German doctor in charge reprimanded him for talking to me. But he didn't pay any attention to the doctor. He showed some real Americanism had soaked into his system since he'd been in the US.

They gave me an apple one day. I think it was to torment me because they knew I couldn't eat it, or for some other reason, I don't know. But anyway, some German Flying Officer in there had several in his pocket and gave me a nice one. While there was no chance of me being able to eat it. I noticed my San Francisco German friend, looked at it longingly. I picked it up, and I was going to toss it to him, he shook his head and said, "if this was San Francisco I'd take it, but I can't take it from you here." I never could understand why he'd refused the apple. Usually, he was a sociable and pleasant fellow to talk to, but he couldn't forget I was his enemy. One day I asked him what he thought the German people would do after the war? Would Germany become a Republic? To my surprise, he said, "If I had my way, I'd make a republic today and hang the damn Kaiser."

I believed he was a German socialist, but he never told me. When I asked him what his name was, he said I'd probably never see him again and it didn't matter what his name was. I didn't know whether he meant the Germans would starve me out, or just what was on his mind. At the time, I'm sure he didn't figure on dying. The first three days in the hospital, I thought he'd be up and gone long before I was. But blood poisoning had set in on him a few hours before I left. He died on one of those days when my wound was still troublesome.

I noticed in the hospital that if a German soldier didn't stand much chance of recovering to return to the war, the doctors didn't spend much effort to care for him. If a man could recover from his wounds, and they thought he might be of some further use, they'd use all of their medical skills to heal him. I'm not sure if this was the standing order or if the doctors just followed their own direction.

My teeth had been severely jarred from the bullet. I hoped there was a chance to have them fixed when I reached the prison in Courtrai. I asked the doctor if it'd be possible for me to have any dental work done there. He told me that there were several dentists at Courtrai, they'd be busy fixing the teeth of their own men and not worrying about mine. He said I wouldn't have to worry about my teeth because I wouldn't get that much food. I wanted to knock his teeth out.

My condition improved over the next few days, and I wrote a message to my Squadron. I reported that I was a prisoner of war and being treated well. I told them I was depressed because I was out of the fight. I asked if they could relay this message to my mother in Illinois. I didn't want her to worry more than she already was. It was enough for her to know I was a prisoner; she didn't have to know that I was also wounded. I hoped my message would be carried over the lines and dropped by one of the German officers. This was a courtesy that we practiced on both sides.

I remember how patiently we'd waited in our aerodrome for news of our men who failed to return. I could picture how my Squadron would speculate on my fate. In the Royal Flying Corps, you don't care what happens to you as much as the constant casualties among your friends. It can be depressing. When you go out with your Flight and you get into a fight, you get scattered and your formation is broken up. When you manage to come back home, you're alone. Sometimes you're the first to land. Maybe another plane shows up in the sky, then another. You patiently wait for the rest to appear, maybe within an hour. All of your Squadron shows up, except for one, you speculate about what happened to him. Did he get lost? Did he land somewhere else at another aerodrome? Did the Germans get him? When darkness comes, you realize he won't be back that night. You hope for a telephone call, or a message about what happened to him or his whereabouts. If that night passes without sign or any word from him. Or if he's reported missing, then you watch for his casualty to appear in the War Office lists. Maybe a month later, messages are dropped over the line by the Germans. They have the names of the pilots killed or captured. Now you know why your comrade failed to return the last day he went out with his Squadron.

A German officer told me about a fierce battle being fought in the air outside the hospital. He agreed to help me up so I could watch it. I thanked him and accepted his help. I watched one of the best air battles I'd ever seen. There were sixteen German aircraft against six of our planes. The type of British aircraft identified them as being from my aerodrome. Two of our planes fought six German aircraft. The fight was so unequal that victory for our pilots looked impossible. Yet, they so entirely outmaneuvered the Germans. Maybe through superior skill, they might survive and win, even though they were hopelessly outnumbered. One thing I was sure of: they'd never quit.

It could have been a simple matter for our pilots. Once they saw how things were going against them, they could've turned their noses down and landed behind German lines and gave themselves up. This is not the way of the Royal Flying Corps.

These kinds of battles rarely last long, but a second is like an hour to those who are fighting. Even the onlookers suffer more thrills in the course of a battle than what they'd ordinarily experience in a lifetime. It becomes obvious that the loser's fate is certain death. The Germans around the hospital are watching and rooting for their comrades. The English two had one sympathizer in the group who made no effort to stifle his admiration for the bravery his comrades displayed in the skies.

The end came swiftly. Four aircraft smashed into the ground simultaneously. It was an even break. Two of ours and two of theirs. The others flew away to their respective lines. The wound in my mouth burned and bothered me considerably. I requested a pencil and paper and handed it to one of the German officers. I asked if they would find out for me who the English officers were that got shot down. He handed me a photo from the body of one of the victims. It was a picture of Owen Wrinn and me taken together. Owen was the best friend I had and one of the best pilots who ever flew in France.

I learned later it was Owen who sent my belongings back to England with a signed letter which is now back in my possession. He didn't realize that in only a day or two, he'd be engaged in his last heroic battle with me as a helpless onlooker. That same German officer who brought me the photograph also drew a map of the exact spot where Owen was buried in Flanders. I've guarded it carefully all through my adventures. I turned it over to his parents when I visited them in Toronto. It was the saddest and most tragic duty I've ever been called upon to execute.

I told them in person what happened to Owen. The other British pilot that fell was also from my Squadron. He was a man I knew well. Lieutenant Renner of Australia. I'd given him a picture of myself only a few hours before I started my own disastrous flight. He was the star pilot of our Squadron and had been in big, desperate battles before, but this time the odds were just too great. He put up a brilliant fight, and he gave as much as he took.

I was taken to the German Flying Corps intelligence department. It was an hour from the hospital. They kept me there for two days. They asked hundreds of questions. I turned over the message I'd written at the hospital and asked to have one of their flyers drop it on my side of the line. They asked me where I'd like them to drop it thinking I'd give my aerodrome away. I smiled and shook my head.

"I'll drop it over..." said one of them who named my aerodrome. I understood then that the German Flying Corps was as efficient as all the other branches of the service in obtaining valuable information. It was right here I want to say that the more I came to know the enemy, the more keenly I realized how difficult it was going to be to defeat them.

I knew we'd win the war eventually, as long as we didn't believe in the flawed thinking that Germans were ready to give up. The Officers questioning me were anxious to find out all they could about the part America was going to play in the war. It didn't take them long to conclude that America hadn't taken me deeply into her confidence. Judging from not receiving any useful information, they gave up. I was sent to the officers prison in Courtrai, Belgium.

BANQUET AT COURTRAI

After being questioned by the intelligence department, I was taken to the officers' wing of the prison camp at Courtrai. An hour's ride in an automobile accompanied by one of the most famous pilots in the world. He was later killed in action. But I was told by another English airman who witnessed the last fight that he fought a fierce battle and died a hero's death.

The Courtrai prison was a civilian prison before the war. Located right in the heart of town. The first building we approached was huge, and in front of the archway was the main entrance. A guard challenged us and knocked on the door of our automobile before he turned the key in the lock and admitted us. We passed underneath the archway and directly into the courtyard facing the prison buildings. All the windows were heavily barred with iron.

After I gave my name, age, address, and pedigree, I was taken to a cell with iron bars that overlooked the courtyard. They told me during the night, I must stay in these rooms. I'd already looked at my surroundings and counted the number of guards. A locked door outside made me realize my chances of escape couldn't be any worse than in that particular cell. I had no hat. My helmet was the only thing I wore over the lines. I had to choose between either going bareheaded or wearing the cap of the Bavarian, who I shot down that day. I can only imagine how I must have looked in a British uniform with a bright red hat. My outfit must've aroused curiosity among the Germans and Belgian soldiers that day. I wore the Belgians cap anyway.

I walked into the courtyard. My overcoat covered the rest of my uniform. British officers sunned themselves in the courtyard and stared at the red cap. They afterward told me, they wondered, who that big German was with the bandage on his mouth. I kept the dead Bavarian's hat with me. But I was not allowed to wear it on the walks we took. I either went bareheaded or borrowed a hat from another prisoner for a few hours each day. The prisoners could mingle with each other in the courtyard. This is where I first learned that there were twelve other officers in the prison besides myself.

There were interpreters who could speak every language. One of them was a boy from Newark, New Jersey. He spent his whole life in America until the beginning of 1914. He moved with his parents to Germany, and when he turned military age, they forced him into the army. After getting to know him a little, I think the truth was that he'd rather have been fighting for America than against her. I learned that most of the prisoners only stayed in Courtrai for a couple days. Afterward, they were taken to other prisons in the interior of Germany. I'm not sure whether it was because I was an American or a pilot. But this rule didn't apply to me. I was there for two weeks. During that time, the Courtrai prison was bombed by our airmen. There wasn't one day that passed without an air raid.

The surrounding Belgium towns suffered greatly. The

Germans had a lot of troops concentrated in Courtrai as well as the headquarters staff stationed there. I heard the Kaiser himself visited when I was in the prison. The courtyard was the least popular place during an air raid. When our airman raided the prison in the daytime, I'd go out and watch the shrapnel burst. The Germans didn't crowd out there. Their anti-aircraft guns hammered away at our planes as high in the sky as possible. It was possible shells could fall into the prison courtyard at any moment. We understood that we watched these battles at our own risk.

At night from my prison window, I watched the air raids continue. What a wonderful sight, German searchlights lit up the sky. The Flaming Onions fired high, the relentless bursts of anti-aircraft guns. Fear crept into me when I realized that at any minute, a bomb could be dropped on the building I was in. But this was the only excitement I was to have. Prison life was incredibly dull. One of the most challenging things I had to endure was the site of German planes flying over Courtrai. The thought occurred to me that I may never have another chance to fly.

I'd sit and watch for hours as the German planes maneuvered over the prison. They must have had an aerodrome not far away. I thought them to be students because they flew poorly. One German pilot seemed to enjoy flying down low over the prison every night. He must've known there was an enemy airman in prison and was impatiently waiting to try his wings over the lines.

I told myself not to worry and knew his day would come. Hopefully, sooner than later. An unusually heavy air raid happened one night. Several German officers came into my room, and by the looks on their face, they seemed frightened. I told him it would be fantastic if our pilots landed a direct hit on the prison. The percentage of injury would be acceptable. Only one English officer to about ten Germans. They didn't appreciate my input. They were too alarmed at what was going on. These nightly raids took the courage out of the Germans. The officers spoke with anger and fear about the raid.

There were thousands of soldiers in Courtrai. Our idea of being able to win the war by starving them out was ridiculous. The food wasn't good, but it was abundant. The Germans seemed to be well supplied with equipment, clothing, weapons and ammunition. The conditions didn't signal an early end of the war. Unless the Germans had an absolute crop failure, they could go on for years. This war must be won by fighting. The sooner we fight and conquer our enemy, the sooner that it'll be over.

We were woke up at 7 a.m. for breakfast daily. A cup of coffee, that was it. If a prisoner was smart enough to save a piece of bread from the day before. He had bread as well with his coffee for breakfast. Somedays, we were lucky enough to have two cups of coffee. I guess you could call a coffee. It was really some type of chicory root with no milk or sugar. Lunch was a menu of boiled sugar beets or some other vegetable. Once in a while, some pickled meat, but that was rare. We received a small loaf of bread—war bread. This was supposed to last us the entire day with the occasional soup.

Our dinner came promptly at 5 p.m. Most of the time, it was just a small jam made from the same sugar beets. Something that they called tea, which you shook vigorously, or it settled into the bottom of the cup. It was really just hot water. This sad tea was a direct blow to the Englishman. What they called tea was awful. Sometimes we had butter instead of jam, and once in a while, there was some type of canned meat. That was our menu for the day. I could eat more than that for breakfast.

We were allowed to buy things. Most of the prisoners didn't have any money, so it was an empty privilege. I sent my shoes to a Belgian Shoemaker to have them resoled. They charged me 20 marks—$5. Sometimes, a Belgian ladies Relief Society would visit the prison and bring us American soap, handkerchiefs, toothpaste, and other American made little articles. These gifts were useful, and we appreciated them. I offered a button from my uniform to a Belgian woman as a souvenir. A German guard saw, and afterward, I was forbidden to go near the visitors again.

The sanitary conditions in the prison camp were exceptional. But one night, I discovered that I had been infested with *cooties*. This was a new experience for me, one that I'd be willing to have missed. Our aerodromes were several miles behind the lines. Our billets were clean and comfortable. Pests like cooties, lice, and any other unwelcome visitors were rare.

I screamed and tried to shake them off. The guard ran in. Right then and there, I got another excellent example of German efficiency. The guard was more upset about my complaint than I was. He thought that he'd be blamed for the cooties. They summoned the commandant, and he was angry. Someone certainly got reprimanded and punished for it. That guard shoved me out of the cell with his rifle butt. He took me a quarter of a mile from the prison. We went to an old factory building converted into a fumigation plant.

They gave me a pickle bath. I washed my bedclothes, regular clothes and whatever else had been in my cell. They fumigated everything. It took over an hour for my belongings to dry. I observed another hundred cootie victims.

German soldiers infested from the trenches. We were all nude; it wasn't difficult for them to recognize me as a foreigner even without my uniform on. None of them spoke to me, not that I could even understand them anyway. I must've been the brunt of their jokes. They didn't hide the fact that I was the subject of their conversation. When they returned me to my cell, it was thoroughly fumigated. From then on, there was no further cootie trouble.

We weren't allowed to write anything but prison cards. Writing was forbidden. We had nothing to read. Reading was zilch. We had nothing to do to pass the time. Cards became our main distraction. And luckily for us, we did have some of those.

There wasn't much money in the camp. I was on a winning streak, not due to any particular card playing ability on my part. I had several hundred francs in my pockets when I was shot down. We held a daily lottery. I don't think there's ever been a lottery watched with such interest as that one. The drawing was held the day before the prize was awarded. We knew the day before, who the lucky man was. There was always a bunch of speculation as to who would win the prize. First place was a small loaf of bread.

Our lottery was played square. If a man was caught cheating, he'd be shunned by the rest of the officers as long as he was in prison. I won twice. A man who, ironically, ate the least in camp, won three days in a row. Luckily for him, his luck ran out on the fourth day because we would have grown suspicious. Even though we handled the drawing ourselves and knew there was nothing crooked about it. He was fortunately spared.

We could buy pears; they were small and hard. We used them as stakes in our games. These tiny, half-starved little pears were worth more than any pile of money. Men weren't as reckless to wager their own rations. Through all of my scheming, I managed to put away two pieces of bread. I saved them for the day when I would escape—if ever. It was not an easy sacrifice. I survived on pears until I finally got one piece of bread ahead, and then I could force myself back on the pear diet.

When a new prisoner came in, we'd immediately surround him. We were eager for any news or information he could give. He'd be anxious to tell us what he knew. If he'd been kept and interrogated by the Germans for any amount of time, he'd seen few friendly faces. An unfortunate private arrived in horrific pain one day. He was wounded with shrapnel in his stomach and back. We pleaded with the Germans to have him sent to a hospital, but the doctors refused. They said it was against their orders. That poor soldier suffered every day and was still there when I left. Another victim of this terrible war.

At one time in our prison camp, we had a French marine and Flying Officer. Another Royal Flying Corps pilot from Canada, two Belgian soldiers, and a couple more from Ireland, Scotland, and Wales. One of the men was from my own Squadron. I thought he'd been killed. He was shocked to see me there. We were quite a diverse group. One Englishman said, "we have the only civilized nations that matter assembled here." They never translated that to the Germans. And it wasn't spoken within earshot. If it had, we probably wouldn't have had such a cosmopolitan group.

Every man would defend his own country vigorously in any argument. I never took a backseat in my praise of America. The Canadians chimed in on their side. We had friendly arguments but were all in agreement that this prison was no place for squabbling.

Every other morning, we were taken to a large swimming pool and allowed to bathe. There were two pools, one for German officers and one for our men. Even though we were officers, we had to use the pool occupied by the enlisted men. While we swam, a German guard sat with a rifle across his knees in each corner of the pool. He watched us closely as we dressed and undressed. There were always English interpreters that accompanied us on these trips. We couldn't talk privately; every topic of conversation would be reported back. Whenever we were taken out of the prison for any reason, they paraded us through the most crowded streets.

The Germans wanted to impress on the local population an idea that they were receiving hundreds of prisoners. The German soldiers never hid their smiles and scorn. The Belgian people were curious to see us. They'd turn out in large numbers when we were out of the prison. German guards struck anyone who got too close to us—women and children included. One day I smiled and waved at a pretty Belgian girl. She replied in German with a smile. A guard bolted at her. Luckily for her, she slipped into her house before he reached her. I'm afraid my innocent greeting would have resulted in a serious injury for her. I wouldn't have been able to help. Anytime we passed a Belgian home or other building wrecked by bombs, our German guards made a stop. We listened to their mocking and sarcastic remarks.

I acquired a souvenir in my time at Courtrai. It was a photograph taken in the prison courtyard. A guard took the picture and sold it to those who could pay. It cost one Mark. We all faced the camera. We tried to look as happy as we could. But the majority of us were too disgusted to smile. One of our German guards in the picture sat at the table in the center. In all of my future adventures, I kept a copy of this picture. Even now, when I stare at it, it reminds me just how lucky I was in trying to escape. It fills me with regret to think of my fellow prisoners who weren't so fortunate. Most of them, by this time, were suffering in prisoner camps deep inside Germany. Poor bastards.

Despite the sparse food and other restrictions we were under in prison, we did manage to sporadically arrange a banquet. This kind of planning helped us to pass the time. By now, there were eight of us, and we decided the most important thing we needed to do to make this a success was potatoes. I had an idea. In the afternoons we'd take a walk through the countryside. What if we pretended to be tired and sat down when we came to a potato patch? It worked out nicely.

When we got to the first potato patch, we told the guards we needed to take a rest, and they allowed us. In less than five minutes, we all managed to scavenge at least two potatoes, myself being an Irish American, I got seven. When we arrived back at the prison, I stole a handkerchief full of sugar. I bought a few apples we were allowed to purchase, and we made jam. We needed bread. We found a German who was a great musician. It wasn't difficult to ask him to play some music for us while we snuck into the bread pantry and stole a loaf of bread. Some of us saved butter from the day before. We used it to fry our potatoes. We bribed some guards to buy eggs for us. The eggs cost twenty-five cents apiece. This banquet would be a success no matter what.

We bribed the prison cook to do the cooking for us. When our banquet was ready, we had fried potatoes, bread and jam, scrambled eggs and a pitcher of beer—which we were allowed to buy. If I'd known this was the last real meal that I'd eat for several weeks, I'd have enjoyed it more than I did, but it was undoubtedly delicious. We'd cooked enough food for eight of us, but while we ate, another man joined us. He was an English officer who was brought in on a stretcher. For over a week, he laid in a shell hole wounded and was famished. We were glad to share our banquet with him.

We asked each man to make a toast. This was the last time that I'd ever see any of those men again. There was one subject we always talked about—what were our chances of escape? Everyone had a different idea. I suppose they were all as impractical as one another. We never expected to get an opportunity to execute our ideas. It was fun to speculate, and we could never tell what possible opportunities could present themselves. One of the best suggestions was that we disguise ourselves as women.

I told them I'd stand a better chance disguised as a horse. Because I was six-foot two inches tall, I'd be more conspicuous as a horse than a woman. Another one suggested that we steal a German Gotha. A type of plane used for long-distance bombing. These are the aircraft used in the attack on London. They were manned by three men. One sat in front with the machine gun, the pilot sat behind him, and the observer sat in the rear with another machine gun. We figured that in a pinch, maybe seven or eight of us could make our escape in a single aircraft. They had two motors and good horsepower, they flew high and could go fast. We were never able to test out this idea.

I thought if I could sneak into one of the German aerodromes. I could wait in the hangar. When a German plane taxied out, I'd rush out, shouting at the top of my lungs and point at his wheels. I'd hoped that this would cause the pilot to stop and see what was wrong. By that time, I'd jump on him when he looked down to inspect his aircraft. Maybe I could knock him out, jump into his plane and be over the lines before the Germans could figure out what happened. It was a nice dream, but that wasn't going to happen. We considered dozens of other ways just like that.

One man would be for trying to make his way through the lines. Another would think the safest way would be to swim some river that crossed the lines. We did agree on one plan to make our way to Holland. But there was one huge obstacle in our way. A huge barrier of barbed and electrically charged wire guarded every foot of the frontier between Belgium and Holland. It was closely watched by German centuries. This barrier consisted of a six-foot-high barbed-wire wall. Six feet beyond that was a 10-foot wall of barbed wire charged with electricity. If you touched it, you got fried.

After that was another six-foot wall of barbed wire. If you made it through those three barriers, you'd be into Holland and freedom. Getting there was a problem we couldn't solve, and we never expected we would have a chance to try.

Mine came sooner than I thought.

A GREAT ESCAPE

I'll never forget the morning of September 9. That was the day I found out I was to be transferred to an interior prison camp in Germany. One of the guards smiled and snorted as he told me that we were destined for Strasbourg. They'd send us there in hopes our pilots wouldn't bomb the prison. He explained that the British carried German officers on hospital ships for the same reasons.

A few days earlier, I'd decided it was a good idea to get out of Germany. One of the interpreters had a map. When I learned I'd be taken into interior Germany, I realized it was time for me to get that map. If I had the chance to escape, this map would be priceless. I asked a fellow pilot to help me get the interpreter outside. He agreed, and we staged a fantastic argument about whether the Heidelberg was close to the Rhine or not. The German interpreter stomped out of his room, waving the map, anxious to settle the argument. After the matter was settled, he went back into his room. I watched where he put the map.

I waited for the interpreter to leave his room for some reason or another. While he was gone, I snuck in and got the map out of the book where he kept it. I hid it in my sock. Only half an hour later, we were on our way to the train station. We had six British officers and one French officer with us. We waited several hours for another train to take us directly to the prison in Germany. During our trip, we were locked in a room at a hotel. A guard sat at the door with a rifle. I wish I could have gotten away right then and there, but it was not to happen.

Afterward, we were marched to the train that would take us to the interior of Germany. There were twelve coaches. Many of them had troops going home on leave. The last coach was reserved for us. They put us in a third-class compartment with hard, old wooden seats. The floor was filthy, and there were no lights, only a dim candle placed there by the guard. I counted eight prisoners and four guards. We sat in the coach as the other German soldiers gathered at the station.

One soldier shouted, "Hope you have a nice trip!" sarcastically in broken English.

Another said, "Drop me a line when you get to Berlin," laughing.

A third one added, "We'll see you soon."

The German officers made no effort to stop the crowd. In fact, they joined in. I called out to a German who passed our window. I asked him if he was an officer. He nodded with an annoyed look on his face. I said, "In England, we let our officers who are prisoners ride first class. Is there no way you can fix it so we can be treated the same? At least to a second-class compartment?" The officer spat on the ground, made eye contact with me, and told me if he'd had his way. We'd be shot.

He told the crowd what I'd requested, and they laughed hysterically. I felt my blood boil, and my stomach stiffen.

When our train pulled out, our guards presented their weapons for inspection. They made a big show of loading their rifles to let us know they would shoot us. The moment the train started slowly on its way to Germany. The thought crept into my mind that unless I could escape before we reached that camp, the war would be over for me. It dawned on me that if the eight of us in the car could jump at a given signal and take those four German guards by surprise, we'd have a chance of beating them and jumping off the train as soon as it slowed down.

When I described the idea to my comrades, they turned me down flat. They said even if the plan worked as gloriously as I had imagined. The fact that so many of us escaping would undoubtedly result in recapture. The collective thought was that the Germans would scour Belgium until they found us, and we would all be shot. Maybe they were right. But I had to try.

I was determined to make my bid for freedom, whatever the consequences. We passed through more Belgian villages. We were getting closer to Strasbourg and the new prison camp. I decided my one and only chance of getting free before we arrived was out the window. I'd go through this window at full speed if necessary. If I waited until it slowed or stopped, it would be too easy for the guards to shoot me. I slipped the window open. I observed the guard who sat across from me. He was so close that his feet touched me, and the stock of his gun that he held between his knees occasionally bumped into my foot. The window was open, and the noise the train made grew louder and louder as it thundered along. It almost seemed to say: *You're a fool if you do and a fool if you don't.* I closed the window. The train noise subsided; the speed seemed to slow down.

My plan struck me again as the right thing to do. I was

positive the guard in front of me didn't understand English. I whispered to the English officer next to me what I planned to do. He said, "Don't be a lunatic. This railroad is double tracked on both sides. You stand no chance of getting away. You'll probably knock your brains out against the rails or hit a bridge." He leaned forward and whispered, "And if you do somehow escape that, you'll probably get hit by another train. You have less than one in a thousand of a chance of making it alive."

He was right. His logic resounded with me. But I figured as soon as I was in the new prison, I would have less than one in ten thousand of a chance to escape. The idea of remaining a prisoner of war was against the fabric of my soul. I looked across again at the guard. He was an older man probably going on leave, he looked like he was dreaming of what was in store for him, rather than paying any attention to me.

I smiled and nodded at him. I'm sure he didn't have the slightest idea of what was going through my mind. I pretended to cough like my throat was irritated by the smoke. I opened the window again. This time the guard did look up and showed his disapproval. But he didn't say anything.

It was 4 a.m., soon it would be dawn. It was now or never. There would be no chance to try this in the daytime. I wore a trench coat and had a knapsack. I had one piece of sausage, two pieces of bread, and a pair of flying mittens. Everything was going with me through this damn window. The train must have been going at about thirty miles an hour. I listened to the rattling noise over the ties. A voice in my head repeated: *You're a fool if you do this, You're a fool if you do this, You're a fool if you do this. You're a fool if you don't.*

I sat up on the bench like I was going to put my bag on

the rack. I held the rack with my left hand. I lifted myself up and flung my feet and legs out of the window and let go. I expected a bullet between my shoulders. It was over in an instant. I landed on the left side of my face in the rocks. I blacked out. I came to and shook my head. I couldn't open my left eye. I skinned my hands and shins. My ankle went completely numb for a moment.

If they shouted to me through the window in those first moments after my escape, I had no way of knowing. If they would have stopped the train right then, they could have quickly recaptured me. But at the speed we were going and in the confusion that must have followed my escape, they probably didn't stop for another half mile. I was dazed. It took me several minutes to gain full consciousness. I examined myself and found that I had no broken bones. I didn't worry about my cuts and bruises. I jumped up. All that raced through my mind was how much distance I could put between me and that track before daylight came.

I lost one of my two precious pieces of bread from my knapsack. No time to look for them. I was free. It was up to me to make the most out of my escape.

TRAIPSING THROUGH GERMANY

I'm not sure where I leaped from exactly. Maybe after the war's over someone will tell me, so I can go back and look for the dent I made in that rock with my face. I didn't stop long that morning after I regained my senses. I bled profusely from my new wounds. I held a handkerchief to my face to staunch the bleeding.

I used the tail of my coat to stop any blood from leaving traces on the ground. I'd walked nearly a mile before I stopped to rest. I followed the stars. I noticed I'd gone the opposite direction, and I wasn't about to backtrack. I kept west for a couple hours. The blood loss made me feel weak and woozy. Before daylight came, I found a canal to cross. I jumped right in and swam across. This swim was a mistake that taught me a couple things.

The first was I forgot was to take off my watch. Even though my watch was broken from the train leap—I had it repaired in Courtrai—I broke the crystal again. It could've really helped me in this escape. The canal crossing ruined it. I also didn't take the map out of my sock. The water soaked the map as well. In the future, I'd make a mental note to take all these matters into consideration. Any future swimming, I'd be more careful and tie these things to my head before I crossed any water.

It was now daylight. It'd be suicidal to travel in my British uniform through enemy territory. I had to hide in the daytime and travel only at night. From the canal, I saw an inviting piece of ground to rest for the day. I limped along as my left ankle throbbed. The wound in my mouth reopened. It was difficult to swallow the one piece of bread that was going to be my breakfast. Luckily, it was softened by the water from the canal. My piece of ground turned out to be a comfortable and safe place for the day. A continuous rainy drizzle made it impossible to dry my clothes.

I knew I had to sleep. Especially since I was going to travel all night. I was so sore. The blood and mud were smeared all over my soaking wet clothes. I couldn't sleep because my stomach roared and ached for food. This already seemed like the longest and most terrible day of my life. But there was still much more to come.

When darkness came, I pulled myself together and headed Northeast. I had two t-shirts, leather leggings, heavy shoes, one pair of wool socks, and that red Bavarian pilot's cap. I still had a couple hundred francs and a little knife I managed to pocket from the prisoner property room in Courtrai. I got rid of my knapsack since I had nothing to carry in it. I traveled quickly, considering all of my injuries and difficulties. I swam multiple canals. I covered at least ten miles before the sun came back up. I found some bushes far off from the road and laid down. I fished out my last sausage from my wet clothes and ate the last of my rations.

The next night I covered the same distance, but the hunger and thirst were overwhelming. Over the next six days, I traveled like that. I figured I was still in Germany. I lived on sugar beets, cabbage, and an occasional raw carrot if I was lucky. One night I laid in a cabbage patch for two hours and lapped the leaves with my tongue.

I had to avoid any hazards. I was in an enemy country in my British uniform. If anyone captured me or gave information that led to my capture. They surely be rewarded handsomely. I had to move as fast as possible, and I had to keep out of sight. Even if it took me a year to get to Holland. I had to do it. According to the map. I was 30 miles from Strasbourg when I leaped from the train. If I could travel in a straight line, it would be around 175 miles to Holland. Now, with all the detours I'd need to make, this journey would be closer to 225 miles.

This country was full of young pine trees and forests. The trees were over fifteen feet high and close together. This was a serious obstacle because they blocked the stars. I'm not an astronomer, but even I can find the North Star. If I didn't, I would have long been dead.

It rained every night while I traipsed through Germany to Luxembourg. I kept up my regular schedule of traveling all night until 6 a.m. When dawn came, I'd scramble to find a place to hide and spend the day. Light woods set back from the path with low bushes were my best friend. As soon as I'd find a spot, I'd plop down and sleep. My wet overcoat served as a blanket. The only real sleep I was able to get was from exhaustion. It usually came closer to dusk when I had to start again.

I'm fortunate I don't smoke. I've never used tobacco in any form. I was paid back in full. If I'd had to endure a tobacco craving in addition to lack of food, it would have been even more unbearable. On the fifth night, I was so tired and exhausted. After I'd trudged four or so miles through the wet woods, I sat on a stump and took a quick break. I closed my eyes, just for a moment. When I opened them, I realized I was sitting in some German's backyard in broad daylight. I sprinted out of there like a rabbit chased by a fox. After I found shelter for the day, I decided right there and then, I'd never let that happen again.

I spent my daylight hours studying the map. Before long, I had it memorized. I soon realized it didn't have all the canals and rivers I encountered, and for the most part, it just fooled me completely.

I crossed into Luxembourg on the tenth day. While they're supposedly neutral, they were no safer than anywhere in Belgium. The Germans didn't respect their neutrality, and If I was found and caught there, I'd suffer the same fate as I would in Germany.

In those ten days I covered eighty miles. I was that much closer to freedom. The constant lack of food, loss of sleep, and wet clothes had made me weak. I doubted if I could continue for long. I kept going. Nothing was going to stop me. Nothing was going to stand in my way of reaching Holland. Nothing would stop me from achieving freedom.

ADVENTURES IN LUXEMBOURG

I headed Northwest. By keeping this course, I'd get out of Luxembourg and into Belgium, where I'd be better off. Luxembourg was practically the same as Germany. The first day I spent in Luxembourg, I traveled all night. I was weak. I came to a small woods with plenty of underbrush. I found a nice thick clump of bushes that wasn't in line with any paths. I crawled in and spent the day.

This sun could barely reach me through an opening in the trees. I took off my clothes and hung them to dry on a nearby bush. I heard a man's voice and jumped up. Several thoughts rushed through my mind. My first impulse was to charge them and sell my life as dearly as I could. I restrained myself and decided to look before I leaped this time.

I'm glad I did. It was just two men calmly cutting down a tree. They were talking and joking with each other as they worked. A feeling of relief washed over me. I thought as long as I just laid here quietly, I'd be safe.

It dawned on me that if the tree they were cutting down fell in my direction, I'd get crushed. It was a tall and big tree and would most certainly crush me if it landed in my direction. I only saw the tops' of the heads of the men working. I had no idea which way this tree would land.

I assured myself I was being paranoid. The chance of this tree falling on me and killing me were remote at best. The men who were cutting it down had to send it away from the bushes, only for the fact of trimming the branches would be that much harder.

There was nothing to do but wait and see what fate had in store for me. I put my palms behind my head and stared at the top of the tree. It swayed left and right. Right when I thought it was coming in my direction, it would stop, and change course. I'd hear the *thwack* of the man's ax against the tree and knew my imagination was playing tricks on me.

A loud *crack* brought me out of my daydream of feeling sorry for myself. Here I was, a fugitive in a hostile country lying naked in the bushes, waiting to see if the falling tree would crush me like a bug. It landed in the entirely opposite direction. I'd guessed right.

Later that afternoon, I heard children's voices. I peered out from my hiding spot and saw the men were receiving their lunches. I was so hungry. I couldn't eat any of it. I thought about boldly approaching them and asking for food. I'd sacrificed too much already—even for food. I'd swallow my hunger.

Just after 5 p.m. it began to rain. When the men left, I crawled out on my elbows and knees. I scoured the ground, looking for crumbs. I found nothing, not even a trace of food. When darkness came, I was on my way once again.

That night I came to a river. I stopped and sighed. My clothes had finally been dry for the first time since I'd began this escape. I was determined to keep them that way for as long as possible. I decided to undress again and make two bundles and two trips across. It was a wide river, but I'm a good swimmer. I could rest on the other side if I needed to.

I easily swam across the river the first time. When I reached the opposite bank, I drank until my thirst was finally quenched and then swam back across. On my third trip across, with my shoes and other possessions securely tied to my head. One of my shoes slipped off and sank in at least ten feet of water.

I had to go back for the missing shoe. There was no way I'd continue on with only one shoe. Diving in my condition was hard, but nothing was going to keep that shoe from me. After an hour, I got it back. That was the last time I ever took my shoes off again. I was afraid that my feet had gotten so swollen, I'd never be able to get them back on again. This time-consuming dive had cost me over three hours. I rested for twenty minutes and was on my way again.

In less than a mile I came to another river, right about the same size as the one I just crossed. I walked along the bank looking for a bridge or a boat, but only found another disappointing fact. I was back at the river, I'd just swam across. I swam across on the bend and I was still on the wrong side. I was furious with myself. Why didn't I pay more attention to the course of the stream before I decided to cross it? I checked the map again and found that it wasn't shown on it. There was no way of telling.

Now, I have to cross it again. I marched into the water and accepted my fate. I didn't undress this time, nor in the future when I crossed rivers and canals. I accepted the fact it was impossible to keep my clothes dry, so I might as well just swim in them.

I spent the next day in a forest. At 5 a.m. I trudged through the woods until daylight came and presented a spot to conceal myself until nightfall. I was exhausted and resigned to a nice restful sleep. Right when the tiny face of the sun should have smiled at me, I was met with more drizzling rain. I abandoned any hope for a dry spot to sleep. The wet leaves fell. Dampness penetrated everywhere.

I decided to wander through the woods in hope of finding a dry shelter. The trees were large, but the forest wasn't dense. There weren't any shrubs or bushes to be found. I got close to the edge of the woods and heard voices in a wagon approaching. I couldn't make out where they were from. My gut told me stay in the woods. Small ditches were dug everywhere. In a dry season they would have offered shelter to a weary fugitive. But not now. They were filled with water.

I chose a spot drier than most and laid down for a nap. I felt the anxiety surge through my body at the chance of being discovered. But the exhaustion took over, and I curled up into a fetal position and fell asleep.

When night finally came, crackling thunder and distant flashes of lightning woke me up. The low-hanging clouds signaled yet more rain to come. There was not one star in the sky. I had no way to tell which direction I should go. I took a chance and started walking in the direction I hoped was north. I should have just stayed put until the weather improved. But my impatient nature prevailed again.

I wasn't sure at all of my bearings. I believed I was heading in the right direction. I had to trust in luck. That night I found more swamps, canals and rivers than I'd ever seen before in my life. I did manage to stumble onto some celery. After a steady diet of sugar beets, the celery seemed heaven sent. I took quite a bit of celery with me. I must've looked like a cow chewing cud lost in the woods.

When I found my next resting spot in the morning, I calculated I'd traveled at least eight miles. Landmarks seemed familiar. I wasn't sure if I was delirious, but I swore I recognized certain objects in the woods from before. I laid down where I hoped the sun would shine. I dreamed my clothes would dry. Maybe even I could sleep soundly. I had a big beet and a large piece of celery. I wasn't going to starve to death today.

As the sun rose the next morning, anger welled inside me. I felt the flush of my cheeks and the racing of my heart beating against my chest. I was in the exact place I'd left from the night before. I'd circled the woods through the entire night. I'd accomplished nothing.

As a consolation, the sun came out and shined on me all day. I welcomed its warm rays like an old friend. I was still so tired. But this day passed better than most. When the stars came out that night, I found the North Star and tried to make up as much lost time as I could. I thought about the many foolish mistakes I'd made so far and laughed. Maybe there was some comedy to this after all. I laughed out loud like a crazy fool. I howled actually. I started talking to myself; I was lonely and needed someone to talk to. I'd have welcomed a snake for a companion.

I ran my tongue across the back of my teeth and had an urge for milk. Cows were few and well-guarded in this country. They were usually housed in barns next to houses and alertly watched by their owners. Maybe I could find a goat? Goat milk is delicious. Goats are usually staked out in the fields, nowhere near as well guarded as cows. I never found a pig, a cow, or a goat. Whenever I'd find a nest, I search it for eggs. Someone had always beaten me to it.

I thought about breaking into a home and bullying my way into some food. But I knew in Luxembourg that the young men weren't forced into the army and many were at home. They were mostly pro-German, and I didn't have the strength or weapons to take it. If it were old men and women, I might've taken my chances, but not like this. Times were hard for me, but I had plenty of vegetables to eat and I would survive. I would push onward.

If I was a better woodsman, I wouldn't have made so many mistakes and could have avoided some of my pitfalls and taken advantage of things that would have been obvious to a seasoned woodsman. I didn't choose this adventure. I was selected by fate to endure it.

By now, my knees swelled, and I counted the blisters on my feet and legs. I'm sure that I'd lost sight out of my left eye. I hadn't seen anything from it since the leap from the train. I can only imagine what I must look like to any unfortunate passerby. Bloody, seeping, unhealed wounds. Over two weeks of beard growth and ragged and ripped clothes.

I'd nearly crossed through Luxembourg before I'd encountered anyone. I walked down a footpath and heard footsteps coming toward me. I stopped. I bent over and pretended to tie my shoelaces. I hoped the stranger would walk right pass me. My luck held for another day. He walked right on by and didn't even notice me.

Following this encounter, I regularly saw peasants off in the distance, but I saw them first and went to great lengths to avoid them. It was the nineteenth day since I leaped from that train, and now I crossed into Belgium. It's taken me eight days of walking to cross Luxembourg. An ordinary man could cross it in less than two days. Considering my circumstances, I was satisfied with my progress.

A HUNTED ANIMAL

I counted three days since I'd been in Belgium. I had one more canal to swim before dawn. I waded in slowly, like I was about to take a bath. I heard a German soldier shouting. I looked over my shoulder and saw he pointed at me. *Damn!*

I ran up the bank as quickly as I could and dove into the canal, swimming for my life. I made it to the other side and spotted a low clump of bushes. I crawled inside my new shelter and made myself as comfortable as possible. I waited. My heart beat against my chest at a rapid pace. I tried to control my breathing. I decided I'd just camp right here and wait it out. I heard the Germans pass by a few times, but they never got anywhere close to me. I was safe for now.

I realized I needed to change my course, even if it took me in a big circle. If I kept heading north, they'd without out a doubt catch me. I walked west for four days. I was still weak and barely made five miles a day. I stayed off the roads and hiked through swamps, woods, cabbage patches and fields. My first priority was concealment. Food was a close second.

I came to the bank of the Meuse river at somewhere between Huy and Namur. I sat in the grass and crossed my legs. I stared across and for the first time I considered giving up. This river was at least a half a mile wide. If I was healthy, I'd swim across it no problem. Staring at this river now felt like I needed to swim across the Atlantic. I looked around for a piece of wood. Something that would hold my weight. Maybe I could float across it?

There was no wood anywhere. I had no choice but to swim across it. I waded in as far as I could until I was forced to swim. It seemed like an hour had passed and I still swam across this river. I saw that the opposite bank was less than thirty feet away. I gasped and choked. My entire body was exhausted. I sank and tried to touch the bottom with my feet. The water was still too deep.

I closed my eyes and prayed. I summoned all the inner strength I could muster. I struck each arm into the water one after the other and pulled and swam. I felt the mud underneath my shoes. I dragged my aching and shaking body up onto the opposite side of the riverbank. My hands shook so violently I couldn't keep my grip on the grass to pull myself out. I pushed and pushed and crawled frantically. I made it. Then I fainted.

I don't know how long I was out for. It could've been two hours or more. The rain beating against my face woke me up. It was daylight now, and I laid spread eagle on the riverbank, dead to the world. I was on display for anyone to see. I had to get up and away. Any minute a boat could pass by and discover me. It was just as dangerous to try to travel. I found cover and concealment in some nearby shrubbery. I passed the whole day there in the sunshine, without food or drink.

That night I realized I had a fever. I was delirious and began talking to myself again. When I'd snap out of it in a lucid interval, chills ran through my body. I thought my end would come soon. After what seemed like hours of arguing with myself in the silent Belgian countryside, my senses returned. I trudged along without a word.

I needed food. I was at the end of my rope and contemplated just lying down and giving up. Why were things getting worse the farther I traveled? How was I going to cross that electric barbed wire when I got between Belgium and Holland anyway? Wouldn't they just capture me again?

I would try one more thing before giving up. It was a bold and dangerous move. I was going to walk up to a house and get some food or die trying. I spotted a smaller house. I hoped because it was smaller there'd be less of a chance of German soldiers being billeted there.

I picked up a smooth and heavy stone and wrapped my handkerchief around it. This would have to do for a weapon if necessary. I pumped the well in the yard, but it didn't work. I walked to the house and knocked on the door. An old lady looked out from her window. It was past midnight, and she had a look of terror and shock written all over her face. She cried out and covered her mouth. An old man and a boy opened the door.

I pointed to my overcoat and then the sky. They didn't understand English and I couldn't speak Flemish. I remembered the word for flyer and said *fleger* over and over again. I'm not sure if they understood me or were just terrified for their lives, but they let me in.

He must've been a courageous old man to let me in his house. I'm sure I was the most haggard and disgusting creature they'd ever seen. My clothes were bloody, wet and torn. My leggings were gone, and I hadn't shaved in over a month. I coughed with a fever and in my hand hung the rock wrapped in my handkerchief.

They gave me the first hot meal since the prison camp at Courtrai. It was warm potatoes heated up in milk. It was the most delicious meal I'd ever had. It was cooked in the dirtiest kettle I'd ever seen. I asked through hand signals for bread, but the old woman shook her head. I'm not sure if it's because she didn't want to share or if there wasn't any. I swallowed the potatoes without chewing them and drank glass after glass of water with a *slurp*.

The woman of the house eyed me curiously. She was well into her seventies and had probably worn wooden shoes her whole life. She had a callous on her foot the size of a half dollar. It looked so hard that it could resist a hammer and nail.

I sat there and dried myself. I was in no hurry to leave. This was the first human contact I'd had in four weeks. I pondered on how nature clothed her less fortunate creatures better than me. I was a hunted animal. Things would only worsen from here. I believe it was the first warm food in over a month that gave me this surge of philosophy.

I pointed to my wet and ragged clothes in the hope that they'd have an old suit or at least something dry I could wear. It seemed that they were too poor to have any more than what they needed for themselves. I didn't press the issue. I rose to leave. I passed a mirror and stopped. I was a terrifying sight. I scared myself more than if I'd seen a spiky German helmet. My left eye was healing and some sight—although blurry—was returning. But the rest of me looked like a drunken and murderous Santa Claus.

I thanked them when I got outside and pointed to the

opposite direction I planned to take—just in case. I headed off in that direction and then doubled back around to make sure there'd be no chance of any pursuit.

The next day, due to the exposure and exhaustion, I decided to get rid of my coat. I figured the less I had to carry, the better off I'd be. When the chilly night came, I realized I'd made a mistake. I thought about getting up and retracing my steps to go look for it, but I changed my mind.

I got rid of everything in my pockets. I tossed my wristwatch into the canal. It didn't add any extra weight, but after a month of traipsing along without enough food, it got heavy. After that, I tossed my flying mittens. My friends used to tease me and call my mittens *snowshoes* because they were so ridiculous looking. What would my friends say now as I buried them in a mud hole. I wore my two shirts that stayed wet and didn't come close to keeping me warm. They were both khaki, but I'd bought one in France and the other in the US. I tossed the French shirt as it would stand a bigger chance of marking me as an enemy combatant in hostile territory.

I still had my red Bavarian cap. I kept it in my pocket and occasionally wore it at night. I was careful to make sure no one could see it. It worked well when I'd cross canals and rivers. I could put my map and other small things inside it while I swam across the river. I had planned to bring it home as a souvenir. But I was determined to discard any and everything that was extra weight. I buried it in a soft mud hole, with much less ceremony than my mittens received.

My hot food experience whet my appetite for more. I figured it would be easy to try it again. I knew that sooner or later I bump into a German instead of a Belgian and I'd have to fight my way out. I needed food. I'd kill for it if need be. Luckily for me, most of the Belgians whom I'd asked after knocking on their doors gave me something to eat. I'm not sure if their motivation was due to fear from what I'd do to them or if the Germans would shoot them for their actions.

On the fifth day after entering Belgium, I rested in a clump of shrubbery as usual, waiting for dark. Off in the distance I saw something hanging on a line. I waited all day, straining my eyes to see what it could be. I hoped it would still be there when darkness fell.

That night, I crawled out and crept toward the line. I was rewarded with a pair of overalls. I put them on immediately and they fit like they were tailor made for me. I decided to find more clothes on my journey through Belgium. Breaking into homes at night and searching for food and clothes was a dangerous idea. I was desperate. I'd take my chances and deal with the consequences. Belgian homes kept large families. There'd be nine or ten people asleep in one room. The barns are usually connected in some way to the main house. Not to mention, I ran the risk of startling some dumb animal that could make a racket and wake up the whole house.

My food search consisted of scouring backyards at night in the hope of finding scraps. I rarely had success. I decided it was a better plan to live off raw vegetables from the safety of the fields. As well as whatever I could scrounge from the Belgian peasants during the day.

Next to foraging for food, I needed clothes. The next night, I chose a house that might suit me. The moonlight shone down onto a barn and lit a path for me. This barn was connected to the main house. I entered and groped around in the dark. I felt something on a peg. I took it outside to examine it by the moonlight. It was an old coat. It fit a little tight around the shoulders and it was much shorter than my previous overcoat, but it would conceal my British uniform entirely.

I decided it was time to part ways with my Royal Flying Corps uniform. I'd literally worn it through thick and thin. I felt like I was abandoning an old friend when I dug a hole and buried it. I thought about keeping the wings. But If I was ever recaptured, that would be a dead giveaway I was a pilot. I decided to bury my wings in the grave with my uniform.

I noticed there were few dogs as I trekked across Belgium. The Germans took most of them, and what they left behind were too old to bark or be bothered by intruders. This was something in my favor as I would have made a commotion cutting through backyards.

The next night I popped out of a yard. It was so dark, I couldn't see my hands in front of my face. I didn't know it at the time, but I was in a little village. I dropped to the ground and crawled along. I hoped to avoid any German sentries. I moved forward at a snail's pace on my elbows and knees. In less than fifteen feet, I saw that dreaded spiked helmet on top of a German guard sitting out front of a little store. I couldn't cross the street. I had to crawl back out and back track. This cost me over two hours of time and effort. I walked back into the night, cursing the Germans every step of the way.

The following night while crossing a field I came to a road. The road was paved with cobblestones and appeared to be a main thoroughfare. You could hear a horse or a wagon for miles on these kinds of roads. I listened for a bit and heard nothing. I decided that way was clear and kept going. When I reached the end of the field, I stopped dead in my tracks. Breath left my body, and my heart raced. As far as I could see in every direction were hordes of German soldiers.

I crouched and slowly backed away. I wondered why so many German soldiers were in that part of Belgium. I didn't waste any time trying to figure it out. I quickly got out of there. I had to again change course and lose precious time on another detour. By now I was used to these reversals in fortune and course. I accepted it as a matter of fact and pushed on ahead. I'd become used to the thrill. If a night passed without immediate danger, I'd get disappointed.

The next night I came to another canal. I prepared to swim across it when I noticed a small boat moored to the side. It was a remote spot, and I didn't understand why a boat would be there. I crawled around a tree to get a better look. I watched five men cross into the fields. I followed them from a safe distance. It didn't take long for me to see what they were after. They were stealing potatoes.

Potatoes without the means to cook them were of no use to me. But the boat would serve me just fine. I waited until the men were deep into the fields and made my way into the stern of the boat. I didn't even try to conceal myself. I knew the men would be busy in the fields for a while.

I pushed off in the small boat and silhouetted against the starry sky was the outline of a German soldier. A feeling of dread swarmed over my body. I slunk down and continued on unnoticed. Either the soldier hadn't seen me or thought I was one of the potato pirates. I counted my lucky stars and resolved in the future to not take anything for granted.

WANDERING THROUGH BELGIUM

I'd gotten used to crossing through canals, rivers, and swamps. The worst thing was the small ditches that were everywhere. These ditches were too wide to jump across and too narrow to swim. I had no choice but to wade through. They were usually the same. Two feet of water and three feet of mud. I could've jumped them if my ankle wasn't throbbing and if I'd been healthier.

One night I came upon a ditch that was easily ten feet wide. I rallied the strength to jump it. The mud and cold ditch water was becoming unbearable. I backed up and gave myself some room to run and took off. I jumped with all I could muster, but came up short. I missed the other side by at least six inches. I landed hard into the mud and water. I was caked with that grimy mud and had to wait until it dried to scrape it off.

The part of Belgium I crossed was full of swamps and marshy ground. Instead of trying to find a cleaner, better path. I just trudged along. This slowed me down considerably and from the *squish, squish, squish* noise I made when I walked, I'm sure I'd alerted most of the Belgian countryside of my presence.

I'd gotten used to seeing a cow and a donkey hitched together to pull a wagon. The first time I'd seen it, I was confused and thought it was a donkey and a bull or ox. But they really did use cows to pull wagons. The Germans had taken nearly all the horses and now it was left up to the cows and donkeys to do the work of mules and horses. In the nearly two months I spent wandering through Belgium, I saw only a handful of horses.

Rubber was scarce in Germany. I noticed their trucks didn't have rubber tires. They used heavy iron bands instead. This allowed me to hear them come rumbling down the cobblestone roads miles in advance. These cobblestone roads were well built and would last for centuries. It dawned on me. This was how the Germans were able to make such a quick advance into Belgium when the war began.

I thought about trying to find a dog for a companion. Maybe I could steal one of the few that remained? The dog could also help me out if I got into a fight. I couldn't feed it, and it would probably starve to death. I could live on vegetables from the fields that were now abundant. A dog could not. I abandoned the idea and continued on alone.

I'd read about making a fire with two pieces of dried wood. I'd never put that idea to the test. I decided the idea would be foolish. Even if I did have matches, I had nothing to cook nor any utensils to cook it in. The air was cool at night. I walked through it at a brisk pace and while I rested during the day, this sun was usually out. Not to mention building a fire in Belgium—one of the most populated countries in Europe—was sure to attract unwanted attention.

I came upon village after village. They were so close together that barely an hour would pass before I heard a clock strike. Every village seemed to have its own clock. I could even hear two clocks striking at the same time in two different villages.

I didn't care about the time. My plan was to travel as fast as I could from dawn to dusk and cover as much ground as I could in between. During the day I had two concerns: stay out of sight and rest as much as possible.

My main food source was small heads of cabbage that the peasants hadn't harvested. All my strength and endurance was due to these dense, bitter vegetables. If I make it out of this mess, I'll never even look at cabbage again. The same with sugar beets, turnips, and carrots. The smell of cabbage used to make me nauseous. Now my life depended on them.

Every night, I foraged for food like a wild animal. I dreamed of finding celery or tomatoes. I was never that lucky—except once. I found a field full of celery and just sat down and ate. My pockets overflowed with celery stalks. I was sick for days—but it was worth it.

I kept my eyes on the lookout for fruit trees. It was already too late in the season for fruit. I did find two plump pears in a tree waiting to be plucked—but only once. The ponds I passed were teeming with fish of all kinds. I'd notice in the moonlight or when the water was clear in the early morning before I'd find my hiding spot for the day. It would be simple to rig up a hook and line. But how would I cook it? It was useless. Maybe if I were a better woodsman.

On a particularly desolate night I trekked through a part of Belgium that was uncultivated and open country. I'd guess it was twelve miles without passing a field or house. My cabbage ration was almost depleted, and I needed more.

The North Star shined brightly and led the way for Holland and freedom, but the path was through dry pastures. A faint ringing of bells from the west and east promised villages, farms and vegetables. The North Star seemed to beg me to follow her. I obeyed.

When dawn came I was out of turnips, cabbages and carrots. Nothing to eat. I needed to find my concealed resting spot for the day. I pondered asking the first peasant I encountered for food—but my gut instinct warned me not to. I went without food for the entire day.

It was a foolish thing to do. The roaring and painful hunger pains prevented me from getting any real sleep. I'd close my eyes and doze off for a half hour and dream of freedom. Then I'd wake back up to the grim reality of my surroundings. The hard ground beneath me. The gnawing hunger pains and the thought I'd never see home again. I'd force my eyes closed and lie back down with my arms crossed over my chest. The dreams came fast, like I was reviewing my life in a silent movie.

The face of that Bavarian pilot I'd sent to his maker flashed in front of me. I could see my tracer bullets slowly get closer to his head. I sat up sweating. I clenched and unclenched my fists. I told myself it was only a dream. I wondered if I was already dead. Was I in hell?

That night I got an early start. The hunger was unbearable. I needed food, and vegetables weren't going to cut it tonight. I'd find a house and get some hot food. I'd take my chances.

I came to a small Belgian house. I picked up a jagged, heavy stone and wrapped it in my handkerchief. I had no problem using it as a weapon, if that's what the situation called for. After all I'd been through, my freedom was worth any price.

I knocked gently. A man in his forties opened the door and asked me what I wanted in Flemish. I shook my head and pointed to my mouth and ears. I tried to get the point across that I was deaf and dumb and needed food. I opened and closed my mouth several times, chomping on air to get my point across.

He brought me inside and sat me down in his room with only one chair. He placed a plate with a knife and fork in front of me. He filled my plate with stale bread and cold potatoes. He used his small oil stove to warm up some milk. I ate like a desperate man who'd never seen food before. The man eyed me curiously. Before I'd finished, he touched my shoulder and in broken English, he said, "you're an Englishman—I can tell. Do you understand me?" He had a genuine and trustworthy smile on his face. I felt I could trust him.

"Yes—but I'm an American," I said.

He gave me a sympathetic look and refilled my cup with milk. I was overwhelmed by his kindness and willingness to help me. I knew the Germans would torture and kill him if he were caught helping an escaped American prisoner of war.

After I finished my meal, I told him about my escape and plans for the future.

"You'll never get out of Holland," he said. "You need a passport. The closer you get to the front, the more Germans you'll run into."

I asked him if he had any ideas on how I could secure a fake passport. He rubbed his chin with the web of his hand and studied me for several minutes. I think he wanted to make sure I wasn't a German spy. His eyes lit up, and it seemed like he'd decided in my favor.

"Call on this man—Johannes Depoortere." He showed

me on my map where this man's village was. "When you arrive in his village, ask for the butcher. He has no love for the Germans and will help you get out of Belgium."

He led me to the door of his small house, and I thanked him over and over. I told him I'd repay him someday for his kindness and help. He'd accept nothing. He gave me his name, which I'll never forget—André Desramaults. I'll never forget the courage and compassion André demonstrated that night. I was determined to find him and repay his kindness when the war ended.

CONFRONTING GERMAN SOLDIERS

Needing a passport would complicate an already complicated situation. My mind raced to understand how this would have to work. What would I do if I ran into a German soldier without a passport?

I decided I'd be more cautious. Even though I now had civilian clothes, I'd been getting into the habit of starting a few hours earlier than dusk and hiking for a little longer than I should during daylight hours. From here on out, no more unnecessary chances.

That night I came to a river. It was about two hundred feet wide. I prepared to swim it when I saw a boat tied up to the bank. It was staked into the soft bank. I pulled them up and climbed in. I stopped. This river wasn't on my map. I had no idea where this river would take me. I hopped out of the boat and decided to continue on foot.

I made several miles that night. Before daylight, I found a safe place in some bushes to pass the day. From my hiding spot, I saw a thick, heavy woods only a short distance away. Even though I'd just decided to be more cautious, I could gain so many more miles by getting a head start. Traveling these woods would be safe, I assured myself.

After spending a few hours navigating the woods, I came to a railroad crossing . I looked like an eagle in both directions for any possible threat. I didn't see any soldiers or trains. I walked boldly across the tracks and continued on my way.

I came into a clearing and saw a small house. An old man was on his hands and knees working in a garden. I decided I'd ask for food here. I figured anyone else in the house would also be old and no match for me. I knocked on the door. An old woman who didn't look a day over one hundred answered the door.

We couldn't understand each other as usual. I did my best through gestures to make her realize I wanted food. She stepped outside and screamed for her husband like a police siren. The old man rushed over from his work in the garden and ushered me inside. They gave me a piece of stale bread —a tiny piece—for which I was grateful.

They lived in a little house that only had two rooms. A kitchen and a bedroom. While I didn't look in the bedroom, I noticed that the small kitchen was dominated by a large fireplace. I tried to make the old couple understand that I wanted to spend the night in their house. They weren't having it. The old man shook his head and pointed to the door. I understood and thanked them for their hospitality before I disappeared into the woods.

The people were becoming more frequent and the population density was increasing. According to my directions from André, I was getting closer to Johannes and the butcher shop in the village where I could get my passport. I ran into village after village. I tried to avoid them, but I'd never make any progress if I skirted them all. To make a mile, I'd have to walk three because of the detours. I decided to try my luck walking through the next village I came to.

I walked up to it and passed a dozen peasants ambling along. I didn't try to mingle with them for fear of arousing any suspicion. Not only could I not communicate with them, but one of them could be treacherous enough to turn me into the Germans in the hope of a reward.

According to the clock in the village, it was 9 p.m. In front of me was a Belgian police station. I could tell from its red lights. Directly across the street were two German soldiers leaning against a bicycle.

I stopped in my tracks. My throat tightened, and adrenaline pulsed through my body. I knew if I turned back, they'd get suspicious. If I crossed the street to avoid them, they'd get suspicious. I was trapped. My only choice was to walk right past them like they were invisible. I summoned all the courage I could and approached them. My heart beat like a drum in my chest. Every step felt like it was in slow motion. My senses were heightened. I swallowed and heard the echo of my gulp.

I was ten feet away. Five feet. One more step.

They didn't notice me. I just passed right by them. I heard their voices and conversation even though I didn't understand it. I walked faster as I left them behind. I tried to make a conscious effort to slow down and maintain an even speed so I wouldn't attract any unwanted attention. I was exhilarated. I had outfoxed the enemy again.

My confidence skyrocketed. My disguise as a Belgian peasant worked. Maybe I could just walk right on by the German troops into Holland and freedom. If I only could figure out a way to avoid any questions and not have to give away my nationality—I'd be safe. I hummed one of my favorite tunes from our aerodrome back in Ypres as I walked along.

I was able to make over three miles an hour in my new invincible state. I came into another village. I'd usually try to skirt any villages I came across. I'd use fields, woods, backyards and anything else that would get me safely around. But I was on a high. I decided to press my luck. I mean—what could happen—I'd already outsmarted a trio of German soldiers today.

I stopped humming but boldly walked through the center of the village. I'd walked several hundred feet when I saw another trio of German soldiers standing at the curb. My heartbeat increased again, and a chill ran through my body. I continued walking. I'd do exactly what I did earlier, and everything would work fine. I was wrong.

I was a few feet away from them when one of the soldiers stepped off the curb and shouted, "Halt!"

I froze. I couldn't feel any part of my body. A wave of dread shot through me. I was caught. Everything I'd went through was for nothing. I was disgusted. What a stupid risk I'd taken coming through this village. Why didn't I go around?

The soldier walked toward me. I had a piece of bread in one pocket and a bottle of water in another. I held up both so he could see that was all I had. He frisked me. What would he do? Place me under arrest and march me to the guard house? Shoot me right here where I stood?

It was my duty to resist. What could I do? I was unarmed and there were two other German soldiers only a few feet away. It dawned on me like a brilliant flash of colorful light. This soldier thinks I'm a Belgian peasant. He's searching me to see if I'd stolen or smuggled any potatoes.

Belgian civilians were only allowed a certain number of

potatoes. It was against German law to barter with vegetables of any kind without German supervision. Some brave Belgians would buy or steal potatoes from the countryside and sneak them into cities for a good price. Right under the nose of their German overlords.

In order to stop the potato piracy, German soldiers regularly searched Belgians at every opportunity. The Germans must think I'm a potato pirate. The soldier thoroughly searched me. He found nothing. No potatoes. He said something to me in German I didn't understand. More Belgian peasants approached, and he walked to them. I took my chances in the hope that he'd told me I could go.

I took two steps forward. I stole a quick glance over my shoulder. The soldier who'd searched me joined his comrades back on the curb. I took another step forward. Then another and disappeared into the darkness of the woods.

My hard won confidence from earlier was shattered. I'd come out of it alright. But barely. What if that soldier had questioned me? What if my deaf and dumb routine wouldn't work with him? If he'd searched my clothing, there'd been a dozen things that would've established my identity.

I continued on, thinking about how important the passport would be now. I'd need something to pass me through all the German checkpoints that were sure to be ahead of me. I debated on trying to enter the next village that night. I decided to continue and get to the "butcher" as soon as possible for this passport.

In the distance there was an Arclight. Underneath were the outlines of three German soldiers. There was no mistaking the spiky helmets. *Damn! Not again.* What should I do? I slowed my pace. I shuffled through my brain for the best course of action. Would I be lucky again? Could I pass as a potato pirate or an anonymous peasant?

A group of Belgian women overtook me, and I joined them. I mingled in with them in the hopes of making it look like I was in their party. We approached the German soldiers. I felt like I was walking into the jaws of death. I tried not to look at their spiked helmets. I'd much rather take my chances fighting these Germans in the sky than here. At least up there I'd have a chance. From here I was doomed. I could only depend on blind luck to help me now.

We began to pass the guards. I held my handkerchief to my face. I tried to imitate the walk of a Belgian peasant. It worked. We walked right pass the guards. They paid no attention to us. I felt like dropping to my knees right then and there to show my gratitude to the heavens for my unbelievable luck.

A few hours later, I entered the village where I could find Johannes and get my passport. I needed to locate this butcher shop. André had given me good directions and a clear description of the street. I followed his instructions closely. In ten minutes, I found one of the landmarks he'd described to me.

I stood before the butcher shop. This is where I'd find help. This passport will guide me through the gauntlet that still awaited me. Through this connection, I'd reach Holland —and freedom.

I knocked on the door.

MY COUNTERFEIT PASSPORT

I explained myself to Johannes. I told him my story, and about how I met André and found my way to him. He smiled and invited me inside. It seemed too easy. My stomach circled in an uneasy way. Was something off? Or was I just so tired I couldn't think straight?

Johannes spoke fluent English. I could finally converse with someone without making hand signals and ridiculous gestures. His butcher shop was filled with choice cuts and the display case was stocked with local specialties. My mouth watered. He told me to pick anything I wanted. He returned with a night gown, a bottle of wine and a slab of roasted meat. He listened intently and interrupted me a few times to express his sympathy. I emptied the bottle of wine, set the gown over my shoulder and dove into the meat like a man possessed. Bits of meat and wine sloshed in and out of my mouth as I continued to tell my story.

"I'm going to help you," Johannes said. "It'll take some time. Maybe just a couple days or even two weeks. We'll figure out a way to get you into Holland."

I thanked him over and over. The amazing kindness of the Belgian people never ceased to amaze me. I told him I didn't know how I could ever repay him.

"Don't even think about it," he said. "Just knowing that I've helped another victim of this war escape is good enough." Johannes stood up and took my empty plate. "You'd better turn in Lieutenant—in the morning we'll talk about a plan."

He led me to a small but comfortable room on the second floor. He shook my hand, and I prepared for the first real night's rest I'd had in two months. I sat on the edge of the bed and peeled my old clothes off my body. My knees were swollen to twice their usual size. My ankle was purple and painful to the touch. I ran my finger over my exposed ribs. How much would I weigh now? I was a strong one hundred and ninety-four pounds when I joined my squadron in France.

When the back of my head touched the bed, I was out. It was a dreamless sleep and over entirely too fast. A soft knock on the door and the creak of an old hinge woke me. Johannes stood in the doorway. He told me I'd slept for twelve hours. I had some energy and strength back. Paranoia flashed through me. What if he'd had a couple of German soldiers with him? I forced those thoughts out of my head. How could I doubt this man's sincerity after all he'd done for me? Even if he did betray me, I was powerless and at his mercy.

He asked if I was hungry and returned with a tray loaded with breakfast. I'll never forget that meal. It contained coffee—real coffee—not the chicory root nonsense from Courtrai. Several slices of freshly baked bread, hot potatoes and boiled eggs. I savored every bite.

Johannes sat on the edge of the bed and outlined the plans for my escape to Holland.

He suggested I hide out in a convent until the opportunity presented itself to make my way to the border. In the meantime, I'd pretend I was a Spanish sailor. I could speak a little Spanish. If I'd tried to continue my Belgian peasant routine, I'd eventually have to speak. He assured me that would be disastrous. Johannes said he'd give me enough money to bribe the guards at the Holland border.

"You're not the first person we've snuck into Holland," Johannes said. "Three weeks ago I got confirmation from a British artillery officer we helped escape into Holland."

I nodded and smiled. Did I really think I'd be the first escapee in this war to get across enemy lines undetected?

Johannes continued, "He also escaped from a German detention camp and made his way to me. His message said he made it into Holland without any trouble. We'll be able to do the same for you."

I held out my hand to shake his and told him I'd follow his directions and do whatever he suggested. "I want to rejoin my squadron and get back in the fight," I said. "I understand it'll take time to arrange this. I'll try to be patient."

Johannes told me the first thing we needed to do was to prepare a passport. He had a blank one and said, "it's just a matter of filling it in." He used a genuine one to imitate the style of the passport clerk. He wrote in my occupation as a sailor, I was born in Spain and that I was thirty-five years old. Maybe with some more rest and real food, I'd get back to my normal appearance.

The first challenge we ran into was the stamp. Every passport had an official rubber stamp. It was like a unique and elaborate postmark. Johannes had half of a rubber stamp, which he said he'd found after it was thrown away by the Germans. He took out a penknife and gathered a handful of wine corks. It took him several minutes and more than a handful of wine corks. The finished stamp was impressive. We were confident our counterfeit stamp would hold up to any inspection—short of a magnifying glass.

Johannes took a picture of me for the passport. He pasted the photo on it like a professional. It took two days to finish the fake passport. During that time, Johannes said he'd changed his mind about hiding in the convent. Instead, he had an empty house for me to hide in. He suggested I wait here until the time was right to cross over the border.

Fine by me. I wasn't excited about the prospect of posing as a priest. The fewer people I'd come in contact with, the better. That night I followed Johannes to a nicer part of the village. The house was gigantic. A four story brick house that was owned by a wealthy Belgian before the war. When war broke out, the owner of the house took what he could carry and also headed for Holland. This house was now used for refugees. Johannes opened the door with a key and told me he'd be back in the morning.

I explored my new home as best I could without lights. It was a beautifully furnished house—except for the half inch of dust everywhere. I counted eighteen rooms. Two in the basement, four on each floor, all the way to the top. My most valuable discovery was the wine cellar. There had to be over a thousand bottles of wine. My fortunes were looking up as I decided which wine I'd choose to celebrate my new found luck.

I stopped cold in my tracks. I thought about the old story of shouting victory before being out of the woods. I decided

I'd wait until I was across the border and free before celebrating. Getting some rest on a comfortable bed would be the smarter choice. I went into every room looking for the best accommodations and was disappointed every time. All the mattresses were taken out, and the Germans had helped themselves to all the silk, cotton, and wool fabrics. This was still a step up from where I'd been. I made myself as comfortable as possible and swallowed my disappointment as cheerfully as I could.

Johannes showed up the next morning with breakfast. After I'd finished, he asked me if I had any connections in England or France from whom I could get money. I told him I had an account in London at Cox & Cox, but I didn't know how to arrange it from here.

"Don't worry about it," Johannes said. "We'll find a way to get it. I need to know how you plan to pay for my services. How are you going to compensate me for the risks I'm taking to help you?"

I was stunned. The change in his attitude shocked me. "I...I, of course, will pay you for all your help." I stumbled the words out. "Do you think this is the right time to talk about this? I've just got the few hundred francs that you're welcome to have. When I get back I assure you—you will be compensated."

"Fine," he said. "You can say you'll compensate me afterward. What if you don't? I want money now. I don't want to wait."

I clenched my jaw. My stomach tightened and my breath came faster. "What do you want me to do? How am I supposed to arrange anything from here? Just tell me how much you want and I'll get it to you when I escape."

"I want £800," Johannes said.

My jaw dropped. I shook my head and spread my hands

with the palms out. "Who the hell do you think I am? Lord Kitchener?" I took a minute to gather my thoughts. Maybe he was joking. I changed my attitude and smiled at him. "You don't really mean that, right?"

Johannes took a step toward me. From the look on his face, he wasn't joking. He pulled a piece of paper out of his jacket. "I put myself in danger to help you. I want to be paid for the trouble."

He handed me a payment order.

Johannes continued, "I'm going to get every cent for my trouble. And you're going to help me!"

I handed the piece of paper back to him. "I appreciate all of your help. I need your help to get out of here. I see your motive is not what I thought." I took a deep breath. "I refuse to be blackmailed. I won't stand for it. Do you understand me?"

"You may wish to rethink your decision," he said. "Before you make a terrible mistake. I'll give you a few hours to reconsider." Johannes strolled down the stairs and out of the house.

Should I get out of this house now? I already had the passport. I could make it to the border and take my chances. I'd have to be creative in the final crossing. *Wait. Just wait.* I won't do anything foolish until he makes his second visit. He still had some of my papers, pictures and identification disk. I needed those back.

That evening Johannes came back and walked up the stairs to meet me. "Well, have you reconsidered?" he asked. "Will you sign this payment order or not?"

I spent the last few hours thinking about what I would do. His demand was so outrageous that I could sign this piece of paper without ever paying him. What bothered me was this man: who'd befriended me. Fed, housed, and hid me from the Germans now wanted to extort me. The thought made my stomach turn like a windmill. I wouldn't be taken advantage of by anyone. I didn't care if I jeopardized my safety or not.

"No," I said. "I'll go my own way without any more help from you. I'll see that you're paid a fair amount for the assistance you've provided." I pointed my finger at his chest and continued, "I want all of my papers, pictures and other belongings you still have."

Johannes shook his head. "I'm sorry to hear that Lieutenant. But I will not return those to you until I am paid in full."

I poked him in the chest with my finger. "Give me back those damn papers. I'll take them from you if I must."

Johannes took a step back and spread his arms in a gesture of fake sincerity. "I don't know how you could accomplish that. Your personal effects are already out of the country. I couldn't get them back for you even if I wanted to."

Liar. What a scoundrel. I took another step closer until we were nose to nose. "I want my personal belongings. You will bring them to me before midnight."

"Or what?"

"I will wait until dawn and then give myself up to the German authorities. I'll show them the passport you made for me. Tell them how you made it. I'll tell them everything. You'll share the same fate as me. Yours will be much worse. The Germans have no patience for your kind."

The color drained from Johannes face. We had no lights in the house, but the moonlight from the window displayed his terror. He spun on his heel and started down the stairs to leave.

I called after him, "You have until dawn. If you don't

return with my belongings by then, the next time you'll see me is when you're confronted by German soldiers. I am a desperate man. I mean every word I say, I have nothing left to lose."

He slammed the door behind him. I sat on the top step. What would he do? What would I do in his position? Maybe he'd march right over to the Germans first and make up an elaborate story to discredit me. Will he call my bluff? I'd never give myself up voluntarily to the Germans. I'd be executed on the spot. Shot as a spy at the very least, probably much worse. But Johannes didn't know that.

I sensed a streak of cowardice in Johannes. I gambled that he wouldn't take the risk of me carrying out my wild threat. He had to believe there was a small chance of me following through. Why would he want my pictures and papers? Was there some type of information in them that would explain his complete change of attitude? Did he want my personal effects as evidence or proof?

Another two hours passed as I sat on the top stair thinking about my present circumstances. The front door creaked open. Johannes walked slowly up the stairs. He said, "I've brought you the remainder of your belongings that I still have. Like I said before, the rest are no longer in my possession."

I snatched the bundle from his hand and flipped through them. There were half the photos, my identification disk, and most of the papers. "I don't know why you want to keep half of my photos," I said. "The missing pictures only have a sentimental value to me."

Johannes sat next to me on the top step. "I'm sorry things have gone this way. I do feel sorry for you and I want to help. The payment order was not my doing."

"Whose idea was it then?" I asked.

"That's not important," he continued. "A proposal was made, and you rejected it. That's the end of it. I hate the idea of you continuing on with solely your own resources. I have a parting suggestion. If you'll follow me to another house, I'll introduce you to a man that will help get you into Holland. He's in a better position to help you than I am."

"How many millions of pounds will he want for the trouble?"

Johannes laughed and said, "you can work that out with him. Will you go?"

Something didn't sit right with me about this proposal. Curiosity propelled me to investigate and see this thing through. I knew I was safe from the authorities because Johannes wouldn't dare deliver me. Our fates were tied together. I told him I'd go whenever he was ready.

After we'd calmed down some, I asked him to arrange some food for me. I told him I was totally out of food since this morning and I was getting hungry. He told me I was on my own. After he brought me breakfast this morning, it dawned on him what an awful risk, he took bringing food to an empty house. If the Germans ever discovered what he was doing—he didn't need to worry about me reporting him. He suggested I go into the village by myself and buy my own food. He reminded me that I'd need to bring something to eat for my trip to Holland.

There was some truth to what he said. I couldn't entirely blame him for not wanting to take any more big risks on our association. I told him I'd gone without food before and that I'll be fine.

He met me outside the house the next evening. We walked to a similar house not far from where I stayed. Johannes opened the door and ushered me into a room on

My Counterfeit Passport | 81

the second floor. Two men waited inside. From the resemblance one was his brother and the other a stranger.

They explained they had another passport for me. This one was genuine. No need to worry about the counterfeit one I carried in my pocket. With this passport there was no chance of getting caught crossing the border.

I saw right through their game from the start. I patiently listened to what they had to say.

"Return to us the passport you've got and we'll give you the real one," Johann's brother said.

I patted the passport through my chest pocket. "Okay, just let me see the new passport first."

The three men hesitated. The brother said, "Not necessary Lieutenant. Just give us the old one and I'll exchange it for the new one. Is that not fair?"

I was tiring of this game. I took a step toward the door. "Let me make this clear my friends. You'll only get this passport from my dead body."

I waited for one or all of the three of them to make a move. I was outnumbered and they could've made short work of me if they had wanted to press the issue. I'd already been through so much. I could taste freedom. I would fight to the death in this room if that's what the situation called for.

I noticed the wall was lined with big pieces of earthenware pottery. I circled my way toward that wall. I eyed them with the most devilish grin I could muster. The room was silent. I said, "I'm going to keep the passport I have. If you gentlemen believe you can take it from me," I patted my pocket again, "You're welcome to try."

I was ready for a fight. Isn't that the reason I joined up in this war in the first place? I came to France to fight Germans and fly planes. Now I was cornered in this room waiting to get robbed by men who pretended to help me but only wanted to extort me. Those vases looked heavy. I decided to hit the brother first. Just one blow from a vase would knock a man out cold. Maybe the other two would run away. I'd take my chances. This is where I'll make my stand and fight.

The three men huddled together talking in Flemish. They didn't want a fight. They made it clear they wanted to talk me to death. The third man spoke excellent English. He introduced himself as Nathanaël and continued in his feeble attempt to convince me to hand over the passport.

"My good man," Nathanaël said. "We don't intend on depriving you of your passport. Good heavens! If it would help you out of the country, I'd give you five. It's for your own protection and ours that you continue on your journey. Without that passport. Don't you believe you should risk your safety before putting the innocent lives of three men in danger as well?"

I'd had enough. I walked to the door. It took a long second, but they stepped aside to let me pass. I turned to face them. "These are dangerous times," I said. "You've shown me your true colors and I'm glad you recognize the danger you're in." I continued, "Remember—if I get captured in this part of the country—they'll capture my passport as well. If that happens, your lives won't be worth a damn. I'll implicate all three of you. My word as an officer will be believed over yours. Have a good night, gentlemen."

I walked out of the house into the crisp night air of the village. My bluff seemed to have worked. I spent that night thinking about those men and what I wanted to do to them. I thought about the Belgians I'd met along my travels. The kind peasants, willing to share what little food they had with a grizzled stranger. How I was given food, shelter and aid from André. Would he have ultimately tried to extort me if given the opportunity? I don't know.

Many Belgians were hanged, shot and tortured for helping fugitives throughout the war. I don't judge them for taking as few chances as possible. I decided to hold no grudge what-so-ever toward Johannes. War makes people do terrible things to survive.

I headed back to the first house to plan my next move.

THROUGH THE KEYHOLE

The next five days felt like years. My food situation was worse now than it was in the fields. I had a good place to sleep but I was still hungry. I had more time to think and plan as the constant hunger gnawed at me. I thought of committing murder often.

German soldiers passed by the house throughout the day. I watched them for hours through the keyhole. I wouldn't dare get too close to the window in fear of revealing myself to the enemy.

I couldn't speak German or Flemish. If I'd try to go out and buy food—even though I had plenty of francs in my pocket—I'd put myself in danger. I waited until dark to scour the streets for scraps. By then the stores were closed, and fewer people roamed the streets. I'd sometimes muster the courage to ask a Belgian peasant for food on the dark, deserted streets. The city dwelling Belgians were much more fearful than the country dwellers. I only aroused their worry and suspicion when I approached them on the street.

I'd be better off in the fields and bushes than stuck in

this city. It was time to leave and continue my journey. I needed to make sure that Johannes and his family would do nothing further to me. Just a few more days and then I'd be on my way again.

When I wasn't spending every minute with my eyeball glued to the keyhole, I passed the time in a top floor room that looked out onto the street. I stood far back from the window in the shadows. From my vantage point—I watched the day-to-day life in the village. I'd pace back and forth across the room. I tried to find ways to amuse myself. It dawned on me how many miles I'd spent pacing back and forth in this room. If only I could've applied them to my journey toward the border.

I watched a tomcat on a window ledge of a house across the street. I used a piece of this broken mirror I'd found to entertain myself. I shined it in the cat's eyes. At first the cat looked annoyed and left. He came back a few minutes later and got used to the glare and wouldn't budge. This was how I spent hours—anything to take my mind off present circumstances. Especially my unbearable hunger.

A few hours later, I stood next to the window. I was hidden in a way that passersby couldn't see me, but I had a view of everything outside. My tomcat friend patted down the street with something hanging from his mouth. I opened the door and ran down the steps. I ran across the street and pounced on that cat before he knew what hit him. I wrestled the hunk of stewed rabbit from his mouth. He unleashed a blood-curdling scream as I wrenched his meal from him and returned to my house.

A sympathetic feeling washed over me briefly, but I had no problem with eating the tomcat's dinner. Hunger took over all sense of logic and reason. I ate it eagerly.

Back at my keyhole, huge carts shuffled through the streets. Peasants gathered potato peels, cabbage scraps, and anything reminiscent of food. In the US, we'd consider this garbage and destroy it. The Belgians turned it into bread. The Germans have turned scavenging into a science. I was fortunate enough to try this "war bread" and it was actually quite good. In my present circumstances, I would have gladly eaten the street scraps.

I followed the path of German soldiers down the street. I noticed that every one of them would stop and stare into a particular store. Nine out of ten of them would stop and stare for at least a minute. Sometimes longer. It seemed only the Germans would stare, but not the Belgians. Maybe it was a book store with German magazines in the window? I had to know what it was.

I waited until that evening. I climbed the stairs. I found a window in a room with the clearest view. I laughed out loud so hard I'm sure I attracted unwanted attention to myself. I couldn't help it. It was another butcher shop. Similar to Johannes, but much bigger and better displayed. The display case was filled with dozens of sausages stacked to the top of the case. This stopped almost every German in their tracks for three and four minutes at a time. I shook my head and covered my mouth, trying not to laugh again.

I perfected the art of catching flies. After I'd capture the unfortunate fly, I'd put him into a spider's web—no shortage in this empty old house. I would cross my legs and sit down, and patiently wait for the spider to come get him. I watched the slow, methodical capture and destruction of the fly and compare it to my own circumstances.

Plenty of books lined the shelves in the house. One of the richest libraries I'd come across in my travels. The problem was that they were written in French or Flemish. I had no understanding of Flemish, and my French was below average at best. I found a New York Herald paper, which must've arrived before the war. I read and re-read it several times. The baseball scores drew my attention for hours. The blow by blow story of Zimmerman of the Cubs getting benched for arguing with the umpire was just as interesting as if it'd happened yesterday.

German soldiers marched down the street. I heard them as close as the next house. I waited for them to pass by my keyhole.

"Halt!"

A squad of Germans came to attention in front of the house. My palms sweat. Fear for my life propelled me. I ran down the stairs. I ducked into the pitch-dark wine cellar. A shimmer of light blinked from a grating that led into the backyard. I crawled deeper in the back of the cellar and found a hiding place. I wiggled in between two massive wine cases. The crunch of boots marched up the front steps, and the front door crashed open.

Orders were barked in German. The *tramp tramp tramp* of men going from room to room made my skin prickle. Such loud banging, crashing, and hammering. What was happening?

Was I betrayed? Had Johannes and his associates decided to give me up? It was only a matter of time before they found me. The Germans would search this house from top to bottom. Only a matter of time before I was found. I could kick out the grate and escape from the backyard. Would the Germans have the block sealed off before they sent the soldiers to the house?

Should I stay put? Maybe the Germans won't search the

cellar. Maybe they'll think I've already left. The squeaking and scurrying noise of mice and rats unnerved me. The banging and crashing noises from upstairs increased. Did they think I hid in the walls? It sounded like they were tearing down the house.

What would they do after they completed their upstairs search? Would they tear apart the basement? What about the wine? Maybe my chance would come when they discovered the wine. I took a bottle of wine in each hand. I would fight. My eyes adjusted to the darkness. They'd be temporarily blinded when they entered the cellar.

Another twenty minutes passed. The sounds of boots on stairs returned. Here they come. No mistaking the *thud thud* on the stairs as they approached the cellar. My heart hurt, it pumped so fast. I felt a renewed strength pulse through my body. A mouse scurried over my foot. Any second now...

"Halt!"

More German orders. The soldiers stopped. It sounded like they marched back up the stairs. Through the hall and out the front door. Impossible. How could they just turn around and leave? Am I delirious? Are my ears playing tricks on me? Maybe this is a German trick to get me to expose myself. I stayed in the cellar for another hour. I held my breath and counted to ten over and over.

I took off my shoes and crawled to the cellar steps. Did they give up? Would this German officer really try to trap me rather than search the cellar? I put my weight on each step gradually. I climbed to the top step. No creaking from the stairs. What I saw in the kitchen answered all my questions.

The water faucets were torn out of the sinks. The water pipes were ripped from the wall. The gas fixtures, cooking utensils were gone. Anything copper or brass had been taken. Anything containing even the tiniest bit of metal was taken. I put my shoes back on and walked into the kitchen with confidence. The German soldiers weren't there for me. They came to pillage the more elaborate houses sure to have metals and materials for the war effort.

The Germans stole every ounce of wool, copper, and brass in Belgium. They'd rip the brass out of pianos. Seriously damaging family heirlooms and prized possessions for even the most insignificant amount of metal.

All dogs over fourteen inches were confiscated. The speculation was that these poor animals were being used as a food source. Another popular theory was that these dogs were "despatch dogs." The dogs wore a special harness on their backs to bring food to German soldiers in the trenches.

I returned to my keyhole observation post. I watched the squads of German soldiers continue on with their work. They marched through the street without singing, laughter or jokes. The war must have taken such a toll on them.

It was time to continue my journey into Belgium. When night came, I'd get bolder and walk the streets—even with the German soldiers around. I'd studied the mannerisms of the Belgian peasants. They walked with their head down, and shoulders drooped. In my haggard condition, I'd fit right in. My height was a concern. I was a full two inches taller than any Belgian peasant I came across. My red hair also marked me as a foreigner.

I learned after the war that the Germans would trap unsuspecting Belgians by pretending to be English or French fugitives. They'd pretend to ask for aid. If the Belgian fell for it, they were arrested, and the German police would be unleashed on them. It was remarkable to have as much help as I did from the Belgians.

I ran my thumb over my passport. It had me described

as a Spanish sailor. Maybe if I could speak fluent Spanish. I only knew a few words and phrases. If I was challenged, and they used a Spanish interpreter. I'd be dead. If I do use this passport—it'll be as a last resort.

I'll take my chances as a deaf and dumb Belgian peasant.

MOVING PICTURE SHOW

When I first arrived into the village, Johannes told me about the star attraction. A moving picture show that was free every night of the week—except Saturday's. He said once I was inside, no one would bother me except to take my drink order. Because admission was free, the patrons were expected to buy food or drinks.

One night while I scoured the street for food, I passed this place. Maybe I should go in and spend a few hours there? I could buy something to eat—except I couldn't speak the language. What if my failed pronunciation gave me away as a spy?

I'd walked half a block up the street, deep in thought when I bumped into a German officer. My eyes bulged, and I made an apologetic gesture and bowed by head and mumbled. He seemed appeased and continued on his way without a second glance.

The next day I laid on the floor of the house. I sat bolt upright. I needed confidence, and this was the way I could get it. Before I'd cross into Holland, I'd have to confront many more German soldiers. To pass through safely, I needed to be calm and confident. I needed to reduce my fear, anxiety, and panic when I came across a spiked helmet.

I'd noticed the Belgians carefully obeyed the orders of the Germans, but they showed no outright fear of them. I needed to forge those same feelings of indifference if I was to successfully play this part.

I'd go to the show tonight. German soldiers and officers or not, I'd sit through the entire show no matter what. Maybe the theater was the safest place I could be—who'd search for a fugitive English officer there?

When darkness settled, I prepared to go to the theater. I had a decent pair of trousers, courtesy of Johannes. I brushed my hair as best I could and with a rusty pair of scissors. I trimmed my obnoxious beard. I was no Beau Brummel, but I fit right in with the average Belgian peasant.

The entrance to the theater was through a beer garden. It was on the side of the building, which connected by way of an alley. The empty ticket seller's booth marked the path inside. I walked in like I'd been there many times before. I was there early and only a handful of Belgians were already inside.

I stood on a raised platform. It was two feet high and surrounded by walls, except for the end where the stage was located. The safest place for me was to get as far to the back as I could. I wanted to be out of the line of sight of anyone watching. I took a table on the opposite side of the wall from the stage. I leaned against the wall. The whole place was in front of me. I saw everyone who came in and no one would notice me unless they sat at my table or deliberately turned to look at me.

The theater filled quickly. Every other person that came through the door was a German soldier. I'd counted over a hundred German soldiers and the same number of Belgian civilians. The first people to join my table were a Belgian couple. The man sat next to me. I had two seats left at my table. I hoped another Belgian couple would occupy them. The thought of having to share my table with German soldiers only a few feet next to me made my gut twist. Every German uniform that walked in increased my anxiety.

Just before they turned down the lights—two German officers entered. They stood and looked the place over before making a bee-line to my table. My heart thumped in my chest. They got closer. Chills ran through my body as I realized they headed for my table.

The two seats in front of the table faced the stage. Except for eating and drinking their backs would be toward me. I could reach right over and touch one of them on his bald head. It would've been more than a touch if I could've gotten away with it.

After the German officers took their seats, the waiter approached. He brought us a program and menu. He waited on the Belgians first, and I listened to their orders. The officers ordered wine while the Belgians ordered *Bock* for himself and his wife. I'd have rather ordered food, but *Bock* was easy to pronounce and the only thing I could say. I wasn't going to push my luck and foul up the pronunciation, marking myself as a stranger.

I'd parrot the Belgian, and when my turn to order came, I said *Bock* as casually as I could. The waiter nodded and walked on. Relief washed through me. I knew if I'd tried to pronounce anything else, I might as well as stand up and introduce myself to the German officers by my name and rank.

I looked over the menu and realized that a glass of beer cost eighty centimes. The smallest bill I had was a two mark paper bill. When the Germans handed a two mark bill to the waiter, he handed it back and said something to them which I understood to mean—no change.

Damn! What was I going to do? I couldn't hand the waiter the same bill the Germans did and expect a different outcome. I couldn't explain to him he needed to come back later when he had change. I just handed him the bill and pretended I didn't follow the conversation he had with the Germans. He repeated the same thing to me as he did the German officers. I noticed a little more snappiness in his voice toward me. I shrugged my shoulders and widened my eyes. The waiter stood still for a second and waited for an answer. When none came, he walked away.

I was on pins and needles for the first half hour. The waves of fear and terror flashed through me like a beacon on a lighthouse. I was never this scared in my life. Every minute of the show dragged on for what seemed an hour. I fought the urge to get up and leave at least a dozen times. The sheer amount of German soldiers were enough to ruin my evening. Once the light went out, it became much easier.

After the first picture finished, and the lights came on, I studied the crowd. From my chair against the wall, I could see nearly everyone. One table had a German medical corps officer with two Red Cross nurses. This was the one and only time I saw a German nurse. It was only ever the male orderlies. Nurses rarely got close to the front-line trenches.

The German soldiers were orderly and quiet. They drank glasses of beer and talked softly among themselves. No laughing or rough housing that I saw. I wondered what these two German officers would have given to know they sat across from a fugitive Royal Flying Corps officer. I tried to hold back from smiling. Then I thought about the huge risk I was taking by coming here. I wondered if it was worth it or a foolish act of pride and stupidity.

When the moving picture show ended, I mixed in with the crowd and disappeared. I was proud of myself, and I'd gained quite a bit more confidence. I could do this. I can blend in with the Belgians, and I can make it across the border. I was getting closer every day.

VILLAGE UNDER ATTACK

I woke up to the sound of bombs dropping in the village. What if one of our airmen targeted this house? I shook my head and laid back down. *What will be will be.* I didn't dare venture out of the house that night.

The next night curiosity got the best of me. I mixed in with the crowd outside. I went from each hard-hit location in the village to see the effects of our bombing and strafing. The crowd outside was mostly German. I avoided speaking to anyone. If it looked like someone wanted to talk, I'd turn my head and stomp off in the other direction. I must've come across as a rude goop more than once. Luckily, I never came across the same person more than once or I could've aroused suspicion.

I surveyed the damage done from our bombs with a technical eye. One bomb landed close to the railway station. If it was only twenty yards closer, it would have destroyed it. The accuracy of the pilot impressed me. Surely, the railroad station was his target. Flying at over one hundred miles an hour and being shot at underneath you by dozens of anti-aircraft guns is a difficult task.

The crowd at the entrance of the station was thick. The Germans paid no attention to me. Finally, I came across as a real Belgian. It helped that all the lights were out in the village and it was a dark night. I wandered from end to end of the village. I passed the headquarters of the German staff. A massive German flag hung out front. What if I could steal it? What a souvenir it would be? I pushed these irrational thoughts out of my head. How would I hide it?

An old woman standing on a corner approached me. My impulse was to explain to her that I had no idea what she said. I pointed to my mouth and ears. I shook my head and made it as clear as I could that I was deaf and dumb. She walked away, but would a suspicious German be as easily satisfied?

I peered into the shop windows and stood next to German soldiers. We looked at the same things. What if I was discovered? I'd be executed for sure. Not only the forged passport, but the fact that I'd been roaming freely behind German lines for almost two months. They would never let me live with the information I'd observed. The stakes were high.

I strolled through a park. I heard footsteps behind me. From the *crunch crunch crunch* noise they made—there was no doubt who they were. I slowed up a bit to let them pass me. Even though it was dark, there was no mistaking the crisp, brilliant uniform of a German officer. The two men passed by me and disappeared ahead into the dark night. It was like I was back at the moving picture show.

I continued wandering the streets. I noticed more German officers dining in the cafes that lined the street. I stopped to watch them interact with each other. There wasn't the cheery lightheartedness that the Allied officers displayed when they were out in Paris and London. They seemed serious and sad. Even here in this part of Belgium, far from the rigid restrictions of Berlin.

Why was I delaying getting to the border and freedom? I was stronger now. My ankle was only black and blue, instead of an angry purple. My knees were much less swollen than when I arrived. I had an indoor place to sleep—for now. My clothes weren't constantly drenched. But I was hungry. I fared much better in the countryside for food.

I was in the best shape since my leap from the train. I was ready. I'd face whatever fate had in store for me. I'd head to the border—and freedom.

APPROACHING THE BORDER

I'd need to slip past two guards in order to leave the village. I'd plotted this out from my evening walks. My observations on the endless walks throughout the village created a clear picture for me. The guards were always posted in the same place and stayed all night. They were relieved in the early morning by another pair of sentries.

The uniform of a German officer or soldier no longer terrified me. I'd mingled in with them so many times that I actually believed I was a deaf and dumb Belgian peasant. I planned to boldly walk past the guards in the daylight.

I walked right past them. I wasn't held up or even given a second glance. The sentries must have believed I was just another Belgian peasant on his way to work. I covered more distance and moved faster than ever before in my escape. I was into the open Belgian country. I approached the first Belgian peasant I came across and gestured for food.

This man shared his lunch with me. We sat down next to each other and ate. He tried to talk to me, but my polished routine of being deaf and dumb seemed to convince him. He tried to talk in pantomime and gestures, but I couldn't make out anything he tried to say. He must've thought I was loony in addition to half starved, deaf and mute.

When night came, I looked around for somewhere to rest. I'd flipped my strategy and decided to travel during the day and rest at night. I was so close to the border. Adrenaline pulsed through me. I was anxious to overcome this last obstacle and get there as soon as possible. I had to confront the greatest challenge of this entire adventure. How would I get through a heavily guarded and electrically charged barbed wire fence? I had spent hours pondering this in the village, and I couldn't come to a solution. What would I do?

I thought about the possibility of vaulting over the fence. If the fence was only ten feet high, it could be done. I remember from college that was an easy accomplishment. Two problems stood in my way. How would I get a pole that was the correct weight, length and strength? The middle fence was electrically charged with two six-foot barbed wire barriers six feet in front and behind. Even if I vaulted over the first fence and didn't electrocute myself—what were the chances of getting over the second? Not good. Even an athlete in peak condition couldn't make this.

What if I built stilts twelve feet high and walked over the barriers one by one? I'd been quite the stilt walker in my youth. If I only had the right equipment, I could've crossed the fences and walked right into Holland. What were the chances of finding the equipment I'd need to build stilts here? Zilch.

The German soldiers used bicycles in Belgium. What if I could steal one? The tires would make an excellent pair of gloves. I could use the insulated covering for my feet if I needed to climb over the electric fence. I'd look for a bicycle on the way to the barrier. If I didn't see one on the way, I'd wait to get face to face with the fence and decide from there.

I needed to rest one more night. I saw a barbed wire fence and thought it may lead to a field. I crawled under it, and one of the barbs hooked into my coat. I pulled and yanked and ripped my coat free, but the ripple in the fence shook for several feet.

"Halt!" The word I most feared echoed into the night.

I was done for. What would I do? I crouched down and hugged the ground. Would the darkness protect me? What if I jumped up and ran? It was foggy as well as dark. Maybe that would be enough to cover my escape. The German came closer. Only a few feet away . . .

I laid still. I held my breath. My heart thumping against my chest made more noise now then when the wire rattled. The moments clicked by in slow motion. The German soldier said something to himself. He made noises as if he— was calling a dog?

A huge wave of relief passed through me. He thought a dog had brushed under the wire and made the noise. I didn't move for another five minutes. After I was confident the German left, I crept as stealthily as I could under the wire. I flattened against the ground and was careful not to touch the wire. I wasn't in a field. It was an ammunition depot. I turned the other direction and got away from there *tout suite.*

After a mile or so I came upon a modest Belgian house. I knocked on the door and went through my starving, deaf and dumb routine. The Belgian woman hesitated for a minute before inviting me in. She eyed me with suspicion but opened the door and motioned for me to enter. She brought me a plate with two cold potatoes and a slice of bread.

From the way she looked me over, up and down, she knew I was a fugitive. Her house wasn't far from the border.

There had to have been others before me. This made me that much more grateful for the risk she took. The Germans watched the border houses constantly.

She confirmed my suspicions not long after. As I stood up to leave, she touched my arm and held her first finger out. She went to a bureau and pulled out a piece of fancy lace. She insisted I take this soft Belgian lace with me on my travels. I had as much use for this as an elephant had for a shaving razor. Her thoughtfulness and kindness moved me. I pressed a two-mark bill into her hand. She would have none of it. She wouldn't accept anything in return.

The Flemish words *Charité* and *Espérance* were stitched on the lace. I understood the words to mean Charity and Hope. This woman must've understood my plight and tribulations still ahead. This was meant to encourage me. I thanked her, and without her knowledge I spent the night in her backyard. I left early the next morning before the sun came up.

Later that afternoon, I approached another house and asked for food. This larger house had ten children inside, in addition to the father and mother. I thought about leaving and not asking for food. How hard must it have been to support themselves without having to feed a hungry stranger? I gave the father a two-mark bill, which he seemed to appreciate. They were just about to eat. I joined in on their meal as if I was one of the family. Our meal was a huge bowl of soup served in wash basins. I hoped they didn't also use the wash basins to wash in—but I was so hungry it didn't matter. I enjoyed my soup and slurped it up like the starving, desperate man I was.

The father and one of his sons of around sixteen had an animated conversation. While I didn't understand a word of it—it was obvious they were talking about me from all the head shaking and pointing. I stayed in their house for another hour. I enjoyed this break from trudging through the woods and was determined to make the most of it.

A young man of nineteen or so came to the door. He seemed like he was there for one of the daughters, but once he saw me he stopped cold in his tracks. His lips tightened, and an overall sternness in his demeanor threw me off guard. He stood in front of me and just stared. He turned to the father and spoke quickly in Flemish. I assumed they were discussing my possible identity and even my fate.

Their animated conversation gave me a chance to look around the house. There were three rooms. They were around fourteen feet long and five feet wide. They had double decked beds in the rooms. How they could house twelve people in that room was a mystery to me. Just outside of the kitchen you could walk into the cow barn. They had two cows. They were wealthy by Belgian standards at the time.

I couldn't understand why this young man was so hostile toward me. I had no doubt he argued against my presence to the family. Maybe it was because I wasn't wearing wooden shoes. During the war—and after— most Belgians wore wooden shoes. I'd never be able to find a pair that would fit me. Nearly all the peasants I came across wore them. The lack of leather made them a necessity. As the war progressed, even the Germans adopted wooden shoes for farm work.

The young man left in anger. I needed to get out of there. What if he planned to go to the German authorities and report me? A stranger knocking on doors asking for food? I couldn't blame him. He just wanted to protect his friends from the consequences of having helped a fugitive.

I wasn't going to take any more chances and wait around

to see. I got out of that neighborhood as fast as I could. I walked for another few hours. When darkness set in, I was on the border of Holland. Freedom was in sight. Just one more challenge to overcome and this nightmare would be over.

GETTING INTO HOLLAND

I waited until it was fully dark. I carefully walked up to the glinting, sharp and intimidating obstacle.

It was worse than I'd thought. This barrier was exactly what I'd heard it was. It was formidable and solid. This wouldn't be easy to get through. I'd come so far—I had to find a way. What did I know about this barrier? It covered every single foot of the border between Holland and Belgium in the exact same dimensions and strength. It was built for three distinct purposes: to keep Belgians from escaping into Holland. To keep enemies—like myself—from gaining freedom through the German lines. And to prevent the German soldiers from deserting.

Just one long look at this sharp, deadly work of art would convince anyone. I heard footsteps approaching. I dropped to the ground like a rock. I crawled away. I needed to find a place to think. I'd come up with a new plan and tomorrow night—I'd cross.

I found a spot in soft grass well hidden in a field. I decided against the pole-vaulting idea. Even if I were a proficient pole vaulter. The three fences spanned over twelve feet. I'd need to clear over fourteen feet wide while at least eleven feet in the air. If I touched the electric fence, I'd be killed instantly. I would have no second chances if I failed.

The stilt idea wouldn't work because there was no suitable timber and tools to build the stilts. I needed to make my way up and down the line of the fence. Maybe I could find an opening? At the very least, I could find somewhere that would offer me a better chance.

I fought against frustration and a feeling of hopelessness. Only a few feet away was freedom. Just three damn fences blocked me from entering Holland. I thought of my plane. I wished a fairy would come and set it in front of me. I spent that night and most of the next day hidden on my soft grass. I only left to beg for food from Belgian peasants that passed by. The Belgians I came across were all skittish. It was understandable. These Belgians lived in terror. Being right on the Dutch border only intensified the fear and foreboding. Nearly every house quartered German soldiers.

I gave up on the idea of approaching Belgian peasants and asking them for food. I not only put myself in danger, but what if my actions led to death of innocent Belgians? I could go back to my diet of raw vegetables. There were plenty available in the fields—just waiting to be plucked.

That night I walked and surveyed the fence. It was so well constructed. I could find no weakness. I walked west, guided by the North Star—my old friend. Every other mile I walked up to the barrier to see if the conditions were more favorable, but it was the same every time I stopped. I was like a wild animal in a cage. How would I escape?

The part of Belgium I wandered through was wooded and dense. I had no trouble keeping concealed. I kept tight into the woods while I searched for a way to get around this barrier. I spent most of the day walking, thinking, hiding. How would I get to freedom?

I thought about making a step ladder. A huge step ladder. I searched for over an hour for some type of lumber or a fallen tree. I needed something to get me ten feet in the air. From there I could jump across the fence. What if I built a simple ladder and leaned it against one of the posts that strung the electric wire? This would be my plan. I spent that night building my ladder to freedom.

I found several fallen pine trees. Some were even over twenty feet long. I took two of the strongest and tore off all the branches. I made the branches into rungs. I tied them with strips from my handkerchief and grass. It wasn't a safe looking ladder when I'd finished. It looked more like a rope ladder than a wooden one. I leaned it against a tree to try it out. It stressed and wobbled. I tightened it where I could. I had to believe it would serve its purpose.

I hid the ladder in the woods all day. I waited less than patiently for darkness so I could put my creation to the test. If it worked, my troubles would be over. I'd be in a neutral country. Out of danger and free. If I failed—I didn't want to ponder the consequences.

I spent the next few hours reinforcing my ladder. I found a clearing of about a hundred yards. I laid my ear on the ground and waited for the sentry to pass my spot. Once he'd gone, I scurried across the clearing and shoved the ladder under the first fence. I followed it underneath, but it snagged my clothes. I wiggled myself free and crawled to the next fence.

In my mind, I'd place the ladder against one of the posts, climb to the top—and jump. I'd absorb a fall of over ten feet. I may break my leg or twist my ankle. If that was the price of my freedom, I'd gladly pay it.

I listened again for the sentry. No sound. I set the ladder against the pole. I climbed. The ladder slipped. Everything happened so fast from here. I moved quick. I stepped onto the next rung as the ladder fell into the electrified fence. The current passed through the wet pine tree branches and into my body. A blue flash. The smell of burning flesh. No pain—just a dull, numb thud. I flew through the air and landed on the ground with a crackle.

I blinked, and my eyes opened. How long was I lying on the ground? Luckily, the ladder absorbed most of the current, or I'd be a fried egg. Fear gripped me. Not the fear of near death by electrocution or of my body being paralyzed—I heard the German guard coming. If I didn't hide that ladder, my aches and pains would be the least of my problems. Again, lady luck was on my side. No moonlight and almost a pitch-black night.

I yanked the ladder out of his path and flattened to the ground. He passed within two feet of me. He was so close I could have tripped him with the ladder. What if I climbed back under the first fence and waited for him to pass by again? I could pop out of the woods and smash him in the head. I had no qualms about taking his life. The only thoughts that circled through my brain: *Get into Holland. Cross the wire. Take your freedom.*

The guard passed by. If he didn't bother me, I could work around him. I'd listen for him and work in between his patrols. I considered my options. I was done with the ladder. It wasn't going to work. There was no way to make that ladder hold. My skin still prickled from the current. The shock had unnerved me. I felt like a piece of toasted bread. How was I going to get over this fence? *Wait!* What if I went under it?

The bottom wire was two inches off the ground. What if

I dug deep enough underneath it I could wiggle through? I got on my hands and knees and dug with my hands like a gopher. I'd gone about six inches down. I came to an underground wire. I knew enough about electricity to know that this wire wasn't charged because it was in contact with the ground. Still, there was no room to crawl through. I had to choose between digging deeper or pulling this wire out.

The underground wire was as thick as a pencil. There was no chance of breaking it. I'd lost my knife early on in this adventure. I thought about hammering on it with a rock —but that would bring unwanted attention.

I dug. When the distance between the live wire and the hole was two-and-a-half feet, I grabbed the underground wire and pulled. It wouldn't budge. I tried again and anchored my heel into the edge of the hole and leaned back to pull. It still wouldn't move. I followed the wire. It was stretched taut along the narrow ditch. No matter how much I pulled, yanked, and tugged—it wouldn't loosen.

I was about to give up and think of something else. I yanked one more time. A staple gave way in the closest post. It sounded like gunfire. I pulled the wire through the ground, and another staple snapped. It became easier. I pulled with everything I had until all eight staples gave way.

After every staple snap, I put my ear to the ground to listen for the guard. No sound. I dragged the wire through the ground enough to continue digging. My fingernails were bloody and broken. Fear washed over me in waves. I was terrified that I'd accidentally touch the charged wire again and get fried. I kept digging. Holland and freedom were so close.

Finally, I had enough space to crawl through. I'd dug deeper to make sure there was enough room between my back and the electric wire. I felt the lace in my pocket that the Belgian woman had given me. I wanted it as a souvenir, but it made my pocket bulge. It could get me electrocuted. I bunched it up and threw it over the fence.

I laid on my stomach and wiggled like a snake sneaking up on its prey. I went under the wire feet first. My body shook involuntarily. If I made the slightest bit of contact with the wire—it was instant death. I forced myself to slow down. I was anxious to get across. I was terrified I'd missed some small detail that would seal my fate. I took the greatest bit of caution I could muster to get under this wire. I could afford to take nothing for granted.

I got through. I was so close now. Only one more fence separated me from my goal. I fell to my knees and thrust my hands into the sky. I thanked the heavens above for my good fortune and successful escapes—especially this one.

I crawled under the last barbed wire fence. I stood up and breathed in the free air of Holland. I didn't know where I was, and I didn't care. I was free. The Germans couldn't get me. I walked a few hundred feet when I remembered I didn't have the Belgian lace. I threw it over the fence. I wanted it. How badly did I want it? It was back on Belgian soil. I'd have to be crazy to even consider it.

I turned around and hurried back to the spot where I crawled through to Holland. I put my ear to the ground and listened again for the German patrol. I heard him. I laid prone on the ground until he walked past. What if he saw the ladder? What if I was spotted hiding in this hole? Could I really be this stupid? I laid there for several minutes. When I was confident he was gone, I went back under the fence into Belgium. I found the lace and stuffed it into my pocket. I scurried under the fence again and made my way back into Holland and freedom.

STREETS OF ROTTERDAM

I wasn't out of the woods yet. I was in Holland. But I had no idea where. I kept walking and came to a path that led off to the left. I followed it for a half mile or so until I came up to another fence, just like the one I'd already crossed.

Wait. The Dutch have the same fence. I walked up to the fence. I could even see the ten-foot fence with the electric wires that had nearly killed me. I heard someone coming. He walked much faster than the German guards I was used to. Something didn't sit right. I hurried off to a road and continued on away from the fence.

I saw the light of a sentry station up ahead. I paused and considered my options. I was unarmed. I'd only be interned if I brought arms into the country. It would be perfectly safe for me to announce who I was. I walked up to the guardhouse. I saw three men in gray uniforms—the Dutch uniform color. I opened my mouth to shout to them. I changed my mind. What if I was wrong? German uniforms were also gray. I could lose everything I fought so hard for.

Too many narrow escapes to do anything foolish. I turned and headed back into the bushes.

"Halt! Halt!" Those words rippled panic through my body.

He didn't need to shout again. I stood silent and still. Another soldier ran up and they spoke rapidly to each other. I couldn't tell if they were German or Dutch. The language was similar, both of their uniforms were gray. Maybe they'd think it was another dog—or the wind?

One of them laughed and walked over to the guard house. I crouched down and crawled closer to get a better look. From the light I saw a silhouette of an unmistakable spiked helmet of a German soldier. Is this a nightmare? Another lucky break. He'd have shot me for sure if I'd approached him. They'd bury me somewhere on the border and no one would've ever known. Even though I was technically on neutral ground and protected against capture or attack.

I was lost. Germans and borders in front and behind. Had I lost my sense of direction? Was I wandering on the border in a circle? I looked for my faithful friend—the North Star—he'd yet to fail me. The sky was a pitch-black starless night. I walked in the direction I hoped was north. In the distance, an outline of lights illuminated the way. A village. It must be a Dutch village. Lights weren't allowed in Belgium in such an indiscriminate way.

I walked faster. I nearly ran to that village. I ended up in a swampy marsh and tried to find a better path. There was none. I charged back into the marsh and plodded my way through it. I was determined to reach this village at all costs. Nothing would stop me. I was in water up to my knees, then my waist. I didn't care, I'd been through much worse recently. Once I reached this village, my troubles were over.

I spent two hours crossing through the marsh. It let me out at the edge of the village. I came to a small workshop with a bright light shining outside. Three men and two boys were hard at work making wooden shoes. I took a deep breath. This was it; I'd make myself known to them and ask for help. I didn't need to explain that I was a refugee, even if I could speak Dutch. I glanced down at the mud caked up to my shoulders. What a miserable sight I was.

"Take me to the British consul," I said.

The men took a step back. The boys hid behind them. They looked shocked at this creature that appeared out of the woods and spoke in a foreign language. After a few tense minutes of pointing, gestures and pleading for help—they realized I was a British soldier.

My new companions escorted me into the village. It was past midnight when we arrived at their house. They knocked on doors and roused some others in the village. Their family consisted of an old woman and her son in the Dutch army. Shivers shot down my spine when the soldier sat next to me. The gray uniform was so similar to the German soldier's I'd spent the last seventy-two days avoiding.

The neighbors crowded into the small house to watch me eat. A surge of embarrassment passed over me as the villagers stared at me while I ate. I must've looked like a strange, wild animal that'd been captured. I shrugged my shoulders. What do I care what other people thought of me at this moment?

I pulled out all the money I had left and tried to give it to them. They pointed out that I'd need it to pay for the train to Rotterdam. They led me to a room where I slept in comfort and serenity for the first time in months. The next morning they helped me clean up and fed me breakfast.

These generous villagers escorted me to the station and paid the remainder of my third-class fare. I'll never forget the kindness of the Dutch people of this village. I'd heard many stories of the Dutch refusing to help refugees. They were wrong in this case. I'll always keep a warm spot close in my heart for these kind and generous people.

A crowd gathered around me as I waited for the train. They cheered as my train pulled out from the station. I had to hold my tears back. Did the entire village come out to see me off? I replayed the events in my mind the last time I was on a train and was en route to the POW camp in Strasbourg. I breathed a loud sigh. How fortunate am I to have escaped that prison camp. I was a free man. Soon, I could send news that I made good on my escape.

On the way to Rotterdam, two Dutch soldiers joined me in my compartment. They looked at me in disgust. They didn't know I was a British officer. While the villagers helped me clean up—I was still a mess. My clothes were still haggard from my border crossing. I wasn't able to get all the mud off my body from the swamp. I hadn't shaved or even trimmed my beard in days. I could only imagine the appearance I gave. I didn't blame them one bit from sitting as far away from me as possible.

When the train pulled into Rotterdam, I found a policeman out front. I asked him where the British, American or French consul was. He looked annoyed and tried to wave me off. I continued asking and asking. I couldn't make him understand what I wanted. I continued to try. Finally, he had a glint of light go off in his eyes. He stared at me suspiciously.

He stopped a taxi and spoke quickly in Dutch. I got in and we were off. We drove for what seemed like an hour. We turned the corner and the Union Jack hung blowing in the light wind—in front of the British consulate.

I motioned for the driver to follow me. I had no money to pay him. Once I got inside, they understood I was an escaped prisoner immediately. They paid the taxi fare and welcomed me with open arms. They gathered around me and eagerly asked questions about my imprisonment and escape. After only a few minutes, the consul-general sent for me.

He greeted me warmly and offered me a chair. He sat across from me and put his monocle over his eye. It was obvious only his good breeding restrained him from laughing at the ridiculous specimen sitting across from him.

I smiled at him and said, "you can laugh. It's impossible to offend me today."

He didn't need a second invitation, and we both laughed out loud. He walked over to me, slapped me on the back and asked to hear the whole story. When I'd finished the condensed version of my adventures, he told me I could have anything I wanted.

"A bath, haircut and a shave," I said. "Also, a cable off to my mother in America letting her know I was safe and en route to England." The consul sent for a Dutch speaking soldier that had been interned since the beginning of the war and told him to get me everything I needed.

I roamed the streets of Rotterdam freely. I took in the air and enjoyed the great weight lifted from my shoulders. The fear of being captured and taken back to prison or getting shot was over. I did have to be careful of the German spies teeming in Holland. Even if they couldn't recapture me, they'd want to know all about the Belgians that aided me in my escape.

My guide introduced me to other soldiers who'd escaped

from Belgium when the Germans captured Antwerp. They were interned because they arrived in Holland under arms. The laws of neutrality compel that they remain there for the course of the war. The life of an interned man isn't the greatest. He can visit his home for a month a year. It's a form of confinement that while not anywhere nearly as bad as a German POW camp—it's still a matter of being held against your will. The possibility of escape is there. But the neutral countries have agreements in place with each other to send refugees back immediately.

I was only in Rotterdam for one day before my passage to England was arranged. I left that night. We pulled out of the harbor, and one of our destroyers rammed us. It damaged our vessel so badly that we had to pull back into port. What if my boat was sunk in Rotterdam harbor and I got killed en route to England? I shook that thought out of my mind. This accident only caused a short delay, and we were assigned another destroyer to escort us through the dangerous passage to England.

I arrived in London. My nerves were shot and the stress I'd managed to control for over two months took its toll. I was frozen in fear. I couldn't muster the courage to cross the street for fear of being run over or trampled. I stood on the curb like an old woman in a strange city, waiting for a policeman or a good Samaritan to guide her across. It didn't take long for someone to come to my aid and guide me across the street.

It was common at the time for English officers to be at home: *getting their nerve back*. An extended time at the front could grind the nerves and courage of the bravest man. It didn't take long for me to regain my faculties and get into first class shape.

I spent the next five days answering questions from the

British military authorities. They wanted to know my observations, and the German conditions behind the lines. A stenographer recorded my story. I told them everything I'd seen. Experts in every form of government took turns asking questions. I spent an entire day answering questions about German troop morale, front line trenches and tactics. Then the Air Corps asked about the German Flying Corps equipment and methods. They wanted to know about the conditions and availability of food in Germany, Belgium and Luxembourg. I'd lived off the land for over seventy-two days. I'd imagine the information about the agricultural conditions were of some use to them.

After I'd satisfied the British military authorities questions, I went to my banker Cox & Cox in London. When a pilot is reported as missing, one of his comrades will be assigned to go through his belongings. They'll check through them, destroy anything that's not valuable, and send the rest to the banker or to their home. If the pilot is reported dead, his personal belongings are sent to his next of kin.

It was assumed I was killed. My best friend Owen Wrinn was assigned with this task. I'd learned that my trunk was here in London at Cox & Cox and I'd gone to claim it. I asked the clerk at the window for my belongings. The clerk was suspicious and dismissive with me. He told me I was a prisoner of war in Germany. He couldn't turn over his effects unless I could prove that he was dead and I'm his lawful representative. I toyed with him long enough.

"I can assure you Lieutenant Ryan isn't dead," I said. "I haven't forgotten my own signature. I can show you if that helps." I scribbled my signature on a piece of paper and handed it to him. He looked at it with his spectacles. Compared it to another signature of mine. He jumped down from his chair and came outside to shake my hand. He pumped my hand up and down and wanted to know my story. Another dozen bank employees joined in and I retold the story of my adventures again.

I'd been in England for ten days when I received a telegram. I gasped when I read whom it was from. Earl Cromer on behalf of the King of England had sent for me. It read:

The King is relieved to hear of your escape from Germany. His Majesty will receive you at Buckingham Palace on Friday, December 7th, at 11 a.m. Please acknowledge.

The letter shook in my hands. Was it fear or adrenaline that ran through me? Why was I so scared to meet the King? I should be excited. It didn't matter. I had to go. The King was the commander-in-chief, and I was an officer in the army. I sent a return telegram that I'd be there as directed.

The time I spent waiting to meet the King was filled with anxiety and fear. I thought I'd rather spend another day in that miserable empty house in Belgium, or another couple days in Courtrai, rather than meet the King in person.

Orders were to be followed and there was no way out of it. I summoned the courage I used in the fields and villages to get back to England. I smiled. I was going to meet the King of England.

MEETING THE KING

I hailed a taxi. After I climbed in I leaned through the window. I told the driver to take me to Buckingham Palace in the most matter-of-fact tone I could gather. The driver made eye contact with me and chuckled. He said, "paying your morning call on the King then?"

I nodded, and we drove on. The guard at the palace gate asked me who I was and let me pass straight away to the front entrance of the palace. I was met by an officer with rows upon rows of medals proudly displayed on his chest. He guided me inside and led me up a stairway to Earl Cromer's reception room. I was relieved of my hat and overcoat and introduced to several noblemen.

I'd heard that before a man meets the King, he's coached on what to say and how to act. I waited patiently for my coaching, but it never came. Earl Cromer spoke to me and asked about my escape. Maybe this was my rehearsal for the King. Retelling the story to Earl Cromer and the other noblemen fueled me with confidence for the King. I had barely finished when a door opened, and an attendant announced:

"The King will receive *Leftenant* Ryan."

I was ushered into the King's presence. If he'd announced that the Kaiser was outside with a squad of German soldiers ready to take me back to Courtrai—my heart wouldn't have sunk any deeper.

I followed the Earl in as he announced me and backed out of the room. The King took my hand and congratulated me. He made me feel at ease with his comfortable and warm demeanor. He asked me how I felt and if I was in a condition to tell him my story.

He wanted to know if I was treated any worse by the Germans because I was an American. He'd heard that the Germans would shoot any captured Americans serving in the British army as murderers because at that time America was neutral in the war.

I told him I'd heard similar reports, but that I didn't notice any difference in my treatment as opposed to any other British prisoners of war. He was a receptive audience as I told him the details of my story. He listened contently, only occasionally interrupting me to clarify a point or ask a question.

He told me that my escape was the most remarkable he'd ever heard of. He complimented me on my courage and will power. He hoped that other Americans serving in the British army will give as good an account of themselves as I had. I'd only expected to stay a few minutes, it was already over an hour. He impressed me as a gracious, alert and agreeable King. We were left alone for the entire interview and I came away with the utmost respect for him.

The King asked me what my plans for the future were, and I told him I wanted to rejoin my Squadron as soon as I could. He smiled and put his hand on my shoulder. He told me that would be out of the question. He wouldn't risk any further chances of me getting shot down and recaptured. He told me if that were to happen I be shot for sure.

I asked about serving in Salonica or Italy?

The King said it would be just as dangerous, if not worse. He suggested I take up flight instruction or serve in Egypt. Neither of which appealed to me. He told me I'd already done enough for King and country, and he wished me the best of luck.

Earl Cromer waited for me in the adjoining room. From the look on his face, I could tell he was surprised by the length of time I'd spent with the King. He walked me to the door and thanked me for all the sacrifices made. As we walked out, a guard and a policeman snapped to attention. Maybe they thought the King made me a general?

I rode back to the hotel in the taxi. My mind replayed different events from the last nine months. I'd been through so much. Look where I'd ended up—received by the King at Buckingham palace.

BACK HOME AGAIN

That night was the first of many banquets thrown in my honor at the Hotel Savoy. I figured my greatest new danger was over indulging in all the rich food provided for me on a daily basis. It wasn't that long ago that I was living off of raw vegetables and the kindness of strangers.

It was time to leave London and return home. I had a loving mother that longed for more evidence of my escape than the few letters and cables she'd received. I told her I'd be home by Christmas.

I noticed a familiar face across the room. It was Lieutenant Harty from my Squadron. I walked over to him and gave him the shock of his life. I held out my hand. He stared at me for at least a minute.

"You look just like someone I know," he said. "Who are you?"

After I convinced him who I was, he continued staring at me and shaking his head. He couldn't believe it. We were in that last battle together when I was shot down. He said the last he'd seen of me was when I had a bullet in my face and my plane was in a spinning nose dive. He never believed the report that I was a prisoner of war. He told me no one could have survived that fall.

After the initial shock passed, he relayed sad news. He was one of the few men still alive from our Squadron in France. He relayed the stories of all my old friends. Most had been killed except a couple who were in dry dock for repairs. He said he was on his way to Australia for recuperation and to get his nerve back. He'd seen over twice the amount of combat I had. We spent hours swapping stories. I noticed he'd gaze at me to make sure I wasn't an impostor and this whole thing wasn't a hoax.

On Christmas eve, I arrived in New Brunswick and eventually into my little village of Waldron, Illinois, on the Kankakee river. My mother stood in the doorway to greet me with a big hug and tears in her eyes. She didn't stop crying for over an hour.

I was never so happy to arrive in a country as I was when I returned to America. Now that I'm back, pieces of my adventure come to me in my dreams. Sometimes, I bolt up and feel around me for soft grass and any sign of a German uniform. I've since learned to close my eyes and go back to sleep.

AUTHOR'S NOTE

This is based on a true story. Lieutenant John Ryan was a real person and these events happened to him. He did not write this book. I gave a creative spin to his story and rewrote it as a memoir to put the reader in his shoes (or lack of shoes). My goal in taking these literary liberties was to bring a deeper level of connection, education and entertainment to you, the reader.

I believe we can teach history from a storyteller's perspective. Instead of rote memorization of endless facts, figures, names and places. Why not show what happened from the point of view of those in the trenches, skies and on the seas. If you enjoyed reading this book, I encourage you to write a review. Also, visit WarHistoryJournals.com to view our other stories.

Griffin Smith
War History Journals

ALSO BY WAR HISTORY JOURNALS

MONGOOSE BRAVO: VIETNAM: A TIME OF REFLECTION OVER EVENT SO LONG AGO

"A frank, real, memoir" – Reviewer

Uncover the gritty, real-life story of a Vietnam combat veteran.

With an engaging and authentic retelling of his experiences as an infantry soldier of the B Co., 1/5th 1st Cavalry Division in the Vietnam War, this gripping account details the life and struggles of war in a strange and foreign country.

WORLD AT WAR: UNFORGETTABLE TALES FROM THE FIRST AND SECOND WORLD WARS

"True Stories of Endurance, Horror and Beautiful Human Beings." – Reviewer

Haunting Truths We Must Never Forget.

Follow in the footsteps of the British, German and American servicemen as they detail the life and struggles of war in mysterious and foreign countries. Uncover their mesmerizing, realistic stories of combat, courage, and distress in readable and balanced stories told from the front lines.

This book brings you firsthand accounts of combat and brotherhood, of captivity and redemption, and the aftermath of wars that left no community unscathed in the world. These stories have everything from spies and snipers to submarines and air raids. A great book for anyone who wants to learn what it was like during the world war conflicts between 1914-1945.

War on Influenza 1918: History, Causes and Treatment of the World's Most Lethal Pandemic

"A remarkable yet frightening history that serves as a stark warning of the threat of pandemic flu." – Reviewer

Influenza should scare you.

Read Into this detailed and chilling account of the Influenza outbreak of 1918. A terrifying virus that stretched across the globe. Even now, a century after the great flu of 1918, which left an estimated 50 to 100 million people dead worldwide, there's still no cure.

This book examines influenza from all sorts of angles—history, diagnosis and treatment, economics and epidemiology, healthcare policy, and prevention, and it gives insights on pandemics.

Printed in Great Britain
by Amazon